DESTINATION

Aha!

Becoming Unstuck in Life and Business

Drew Gerber

First Edition, August 2013

Wasabi Publicity, Inc.
790 Thompson Road
Saluda, NC 28773

Published in the United States by The Art of Aha! Publishing, a division of Wasabi Publicity, Inc., Saluda, North Carolina.

ISBN: 978-0-9894575-0-7

Printed in the United States of America

CONTENTS

FOREWORD

Do me a favor. Before reading anything else, ask yourself this question:

What am I doing to protect my dreams?

If your answer is nonexistent because you can't articulate your dreams, or your answer doesn't hold muster because those dreams are wholly unreasonable, then it's time pivot and to get to work. And that all begins the minute you pick up this book.

Drew Gerber and I met more than a dozen years ago at an educational course aimed at providing us with *some* of the tools necessary for personal growth and development. At the time, Drew was just another face in the crowd. Together, we listened and took notes and participated over the course of the four-day program. Little did I know that Drew — as

charismatic and genuine a person as you'll ever meet — was on

his way to doing so much more than just answering the

question for himself: How do I become unstuck?

While the inconvenience of becoming mired in the mayhem of

life probably hasn't waned since the beginning of time, the

demand for an easy-to-read primer on becoming unstuck so

you can pursue your dreams has dramatically increased. Walk

into any bookstore and make your way to the self-help section

and you'll find shelf after shelf of titles that claim to provide a

panacea for getting you off your keister and attaining that for

which you believe you were intended. In the business category,

I've found few titles that approach the subject in a truly helpful,

meaningful, and concrete way.

Here, in *Destination Aha! Becoming Unstuck in Life and

Business*, Drew Gerber goes beyond the Pollyannaish clichés

we're used to reading in books about moving forward and

pursuing our dreams. Instead, it provides you with the must-have tools necessary for moving on when feeling stuck. In most cases, it turns out that "being down so long it looks like up to me" isn't the result of where you are. It's because of where you were and what you overlooked or failed to do while you were there.

That's why, when you're stuck in business or in your personal life, it's critically important that you return to the basics and examine — maybe for the first time —your purpose, values, mission, goals, and dreams.

The author and cartoonist Hugh MacLeod once wrote: "Everybody has their own private Mount Everest they were put on this earth to climb. You may never reach the summit; for that you will be forgiven. But if you don't make at least one serious attempt to get above the snow line, years later you will find yourself lying on your deathbed, and all you will feel is emptiness."

In your quest to reach the summit, be sure to pack and read this book. *Destination Aha! Becoming Unstuck in Life and Business* is well worth the extra weight it adds to your arsenal of must-have tools and equipment.

— Mikal E. Belicove
Columnist & Contributing Author
Entrepreneur Magazine

INTRODUCTION

Naked.

What better way to start this book than with the image of me naked, sitting in a lithium-infused hot pot with a bunch of naked hippies.

I'm not talking about the hot pots Chinese cooks use to stew fabulous concoctions, but the natural hot springs that I grew up with in Utah. My parents would say, "We're going to Lava, Idaho to soak in the hot pots." And that expression stuck. The labeling is irrelevant, as it is with most things. All you need to know is that I am naked in a hot pool of water with a bunch of middle-aged hippies. Isn't this a perfect place to begin a book about getting you and your business unstuck?

While my being naked might be of interest to you, I really don't think it is going to get you unstuck. Fortunately (for both of us), there is more to this story.

It began when I was working for a dot com in Denver right after the tech bubble popped. At that point, it became pretty clear that this was no place for a young, brilliant entrepreneur (yes, me!) to be hanging out. I had originally moved to Denver to be a computer developer, as programming was something that I did while getting my degree in chemical engineering. But it didn't take long after arriving at Dream Team Technologies to realize that I was not cut out to be a program developer. It just wasn't my cup of tea to sit at a computer, slogging hour after hour trying to find a line of code that threw a computer off. So I bounced around the company in the hopes of finding the perfect fit for me. But after a while, the writing on the wall was clear: nothing was right.

I needed a place to find myself and to sort out my life. Some people around the office talked about an incredible spot near

Crestone, Colorado in the foothills of the Sangre de Cristo

Mountains, complete with lithium-infused hot pots and the

most amazing vistas. Shirley MacLaine, whom I adore, owned a

plot of land in the area and wrote about UFO sightings and

vortexes. I was already intrigued, but this sealed the deal.

Ready to take on a strange, new adventure I loaded up my

Volkswagen and headed to Crestone, Colorado, to seek the

lithium-infused hot water, UFOs, and a sense of direction. I

landed at Valley View, an oasis perched high above the

northern San Luis Valley where both your cares and your

clothes where optional (which explains the naked hippies.)

"Clothing optional" gave me a moment of pause. I was already

on my way to find myself, so why not do it naked?

On the first day of looking for myself and my destiny, naked in

a lithium-infused hot pot, I found myself sitting across from a

bearded astrologer as he read people's astrological charts. As

fascinating as it was, I wasn't interested in hearing other

people's destinies. I had enough trouble discovering my own. I did my best to block out the conversation, but something caught my attention and I suddenly locked eyes with the astrologer. Did he sense my confused and wandering mind? He asked me when my birthday was. Normally I wouldn't divulge all my personal info to anyone, especially a naked hippy. But for some reason, it just seemed like the right thing to do – weird right? Amazingly, he began to explain exactly what was going on in my life. I have always been a fan of astrology, but this made me a true believer. It was as if he had literally just recited a book of my life to me.

As the night went on, people exited the pool until the only ones left were the bearded astrologer, his girlfriend and me. Nonchalantly, the girlfriend turned to me and asked, "We're going to the Tibetan Stupa tomorrow. Want to come?"

Of course, I had no clue what the heck a Tibetan Stupa was. So rather than admit it, I accepted the invitation. We said our goodnights, set a time to meet in the morning, and I was off to bed.

We met first thing the next morning and I decided to follow them in my Volkswagen. (They had a small truck and, although we had been naked together, that seemed a little too intimate.) After driving on various different main roads, we eventually hit a dirt road. I noticed my guides in their truck fishtailed a little bit in the dirt. I didn't know how my new Volkswagen would handle off-road, but I took the risk and went for it – in retrospect, not the best idea. A bit too confident in my car's abilities, I got myself stuck in the sand.

I revved the engine repeatedly. The more I tried to get unstuck, the deeper my car got stuck in the sand. And I realized that this wasn't new for me, literally or metaphorically. It was actually a very familiar feeling. I had spent a lot of my life stuck in the slippery sandpit of my mind, feverishly trying to get unstuck and think my way out of my annoyingly repetitive thoughts. It wasn't until I was in college that I learned the name for my kind of mental stuckness: OCD (Obsessive Compulsive Disorder). Back then, I certainly didn't consider my OCD a gift.

But today, I see the insight that OCD has given me, insight into how we as human beings get ourselves stuck.

But there I was in my Volkswagen, in that same repetitive cycle: throw it in reverse, throw it in first, throw it in reverse, throw it in first – then repeat. Finally, Mr. Astrologer ran from his truck, yelling and waving his arms for me to stop. At this point, I felt hopelessly defeated by the situation and had no idea how I was going to get out of it.

While I sat there in frustration, my hippy friend's girlfriend started talking about the philosophy of Buddhism. You'd think this would further annoy me, considering that my car was stuck up to its bumpers in sand. But weirdly enough, it calmed me down. I started to feel more... I guess you would call it, present in the moment. It was right then, when my focus wasn't on my frustration or my car or the sand, that my eyes were able to see what was right in front of me: one of most beautiful vistas I have ever seen.

Suddenly, my attention turned when a monk, riding a bicycle with a basket, came pedaling down the dirt road. Later on I learned about the Buddhist monastery further down the road. But at that very moment, it was all so bizarre – and oddly inspiring. In that moment, I was able to take everything in. I just began to breathe and get in the flow of life. A few peaceful moments later, a four-wheel drive truck came whizzing down the dirt road. And lo and behold, this four-wheel drive just happened to have a winch that could get my Volkswagen out of the sand!

That was one of my defining moments. It was then that I learned that, when we become aware and present, signs appear before us to let us know that we're fishtailing or stuck. It wasn't just my car that was stuck in the sand. I was stuck, mentally stuck, in all my frustration. In that precious moment, I realized that the secret to getting unstuck in life is to quit resisting and to just get into the flow of things. Once you open your eyes to the problem, the solutions will reveal themselves.

My commitment in writing this book is to have you quit trying to get unstuck from the sand and position yourself to let the universe pull you out. This is not new information, but information many of us have just forgotten. I'd like to help you remember.

Fishtailing (How to Recognize You're Stuck)

Stuck or not stuck . . . that is the question.

From the very beginning of my PR firm, Wasabi Publicity, up until now, I've been no stranger to being stuck. As I look back on those different "stuck" experiences, it all seems pretty obvious why and how they all happened. But at the time, none of that ever occurred to me. I knew everyone naturally experiences obstacles during their lifetime. But I later realized that being stuck is a state that people accidently *drive* themselves into.

It's like my being stuck in the sand in my VW. Out of pure fury, fire, and frustration of being stuck in the sand, I furiously floored my gas pedal and revved my engine – neither of which resulted in movement. All I did was dig a deeper hole that made me more stuck. Why didn't I just stop when I knew I wasn't making any progress? Everything I did drove me deeper into the quicksand. Was it my mindset at the time or were my emotions getting the better of me? Was I taking the wrong approach, using the wrong equipment? It was probably all of that, because all of those things play a role in the larger state of being stuck.

This book is designed not only to help you know when you are stuck, but also to help you spot the warning signs, the "pre-stuck symptoms." Will having this knowledge mean you'll never be stuck again? Not necessarily. But that's a good thing. We learn from our experiences and sometimes the universe needs to dish out some curve balls to keep us on our toes. It's those experiences that lead to some of our greatest life lessons. However, we can certainly shorten the cycle of stuckness so we can move on to new and improved lessons!

Clues That You're Stuck

"But, hey! I already know when I'm stuck." Really? Have you noticed how easy it is to spot someone else banging his head up against a wall or spinning her wheels in the sand? What is easy to detect in others is not so easy to pinpoint in ourselves. You know what I'm talking about. It's a part of our human nature. We're wired to think that we're running pretty smoothly. But that other guy? It's clear to us when he's not firing on all cylinders. Maybe that's why it's so easy for us to give advice, but difficult to take it – even our own! We never want to take a spoon of our own medicine. Isn't this why people love TV shows and movies so much? We watch others flailing around, making mistakes and mock them for being so ignorant. I can hear myself clearly: "Don't go in there, you moron! There's obviously a cannibalistic, crazy person about to eat you!" or "He's obviously cheating on you, sweetheart. Get the hint." We feel like we have a step up on the other person because it seems *so obvious.*

But you can't get unstuck if you don't recognize that you are stuck in the first place. And all you have to do now to recognize your areas of stuckness is to take a cold, hard look in the mirror, pay attention to what you see and feel, and 'fess up to what's there. You may not have known that you're stuck. You may be unconscious of the fact. The only way to really know if you are stuck is to look for the signs. I like to think of them as the road signs of life. If you pay attention to these signs, they'll guide you along the right path and tell you when you're off that path. For me, the signs that are most important are thoughts, feelings, energy, and the results around me.

Does any of the following sound familiar?

You feel uninspired. You wake up in the morning and just don't feel jazzed about the day ahead. When someone asks you what's going on with your business, you reply, "Oh, you know. Same old same old." You don't feel bad – but you don't feel as good as you once felt working your business. We have this preconception that stuck means you don't have results, but stuck is an energetic state of being. You can be successful in what you do and still be stuck.

You're busy, you're getting some results, but the scenery doesn't change. You think you're doing everything you are supposed to be doing, but you're bored and asking, "Is there more to it than this?"

It's happening, but it doesn't feel good. It's all coming together. You're reaching the goals you set and you're seeing results. Your vision seems to be manifesting, maybe exactly as you hoped it would. But somehow, it just doesn't feel good. You feel antsy, frustrated, maybe anxious, generally pissy – but you can't explain it. Everything is going so right, so why does it feel so wrong? That vague sense of disconnect and discomfort is oftentimes the harbinger of a more deep set and internalized unhappiness. Matthew B. James, one of my clients, is a lifelong student and present-day teacher of Huna, an ancient Hawaiian philosophy. He says anxiety is a "signal from your unconscious that you're not focusing on the things that are important to you." In other words, anxiety is one of the sure fire indicators that you are stuck.

Your subconscious is giving you other signals. The role of the subconscious mind is to signal you when something's going on that you aren't paying attention to. And the main vehicles the subconscious uses are your emotions and your body. Your body tells you when you are heading down the wrong path, often even signaling that information before your mind can label it. For me, I know that I am out of whack when I start clenching my jaw and sensing a tightness in my chest. A shallowness of breath is incredibly common, which makes sense, as breath is the essence of life. Or you may feel constantly tired, run down. It could appear as tense neck and shoulders, frequent stomachaches, or headaches that can't be explained. Any of these physical symptoms can be signals from the subconscious that you're stuck and something needs to give.

And your emotions? Haven't most of us had that experience of, "I don't know why, but I just feel sad lately"? Or you could feel nervous, angry, depressed, anxious – any number of feelings that don't have an obvious source. In contemporary life, I think there's a lot of low-grade depression (often masked as apathy) along with the ubiquitous stress we've become so familiar with. If you can't connect these feelings to a particular situation, odds are your subconscious is trying to signal you.

Your mind keeps spinning. Have you become indecisive, constantly second guessing yourself? Paralysis by analysis? Entrepreneurs are smart rats. I know because I'm one of you! If you couple that with OCD, it's truly a winning formula for being stuck. You know that old saying that we teach what we need to learn? Hello!

We're confident that we can think our way out of any situation and that's where we get into trouble. All these things may be running through our heads: Should I change my website? Spend more time on Twitter? Hire an assistant? Write a book?

You get the point. We get caught up in an overwhelming cycle of overthinking. We live in a society that stakes such a high value on thinking. From a very early age, we're taught to think our way out of any situation and to strategize to get the things we want. Even our school systems train us to think about how to plan our whole way through life and how to be smarter than the next guy. Being trapped in our heads with all this thinking, we might actually miss the signs. Rather than gaining direction, we get pushed off the track and our overactive minds send us into a swirl.

It's not happening fast enough. I am not talking about impatience here— when you want something to happen right now, this very minute. Despite our microwave, fast food, overnight success culture, we do live on a plane that has time as one of its components. Things take time and I believe that everything happens for a reason and exactly when it's supposed to happen. But even knowing that, you might have the instinct or intuition that things are not moving as quickly as they are divinely ordered to be moving. You know that famous saying that it takes 10 years to be an overnight sensation? We often forget about the 10-year part.

How it's always worked isn't working. One reason we entrepreneurs get stuck is that we're really smart rats and we have figured out how to get the cheese! But when someone (or the economy or technology or current market trends) moves that cheese, your old strategies may no longer work. Are you putting in the work, doing what you've always done, but not getting the results you've always gotten?

There's an analogy from whitewater kayaking that describes this kind of stuck. Imagine yourself kayaking down a river when, at some point, you get caught in an eddy that leaves you swirling around and around. Like kayakers, entrepreneurs will get stuck in a rut where they are taking action but making no progress. Like being in an eddy, they may be paddling like crazy but at a standstill. It's times like these when entrepreneurs think they're still being competitive, but really are only doing business. In the business world, this is being stuck. Entrepreneurs often find themselves in the eddy of the stream – paddling round and round in the same place without really knowing it.

Your relationships are off kilter. Sometimes being stuck show up in how people are reacting and interacting with you. If co-workers, family, or friends seem upset or irritated by you (or you feel uncharacteristically upset or irritated by them), you might be stuck without knowing it. Maybe suddenly, you find yourself surrounded by personal drama and misunderstanding. Conversations that used to be easy are difficult. Collaborations that used to be smooth are bumpy. Your external environment and relationships are always a reflection of your own state. So if your external environment and relationships are suddenly not working as they used to, it's time to look to see if the problem is you and some form of stuckness.

A sure sign that you're stuck is if you think you are NOT the reason your business is not successful. The ultimate sign of being stuck is pointing your finger anywhere but at yourself. I know, sorry about that. But one of the reasons that we're entrepreneurs is because we love to play our own game, right? We make up the rules. Well, if you made up the rules and you're *not* winning the game, whose fault is that? See my point? Here's a great example.

Take this client that we're currently working with. They are one of my favorite clients and have been with us for years. They recently switched their business model to do more internet marketing, so we've been helping them with an internet marketing campaign and we've been getting some good results.

But, *not* the results they were looking for—and we all know what happens when we don't get what we want in life, right? We get upset.

They started accusing us of not following through with this and that. (If there's one thing my team does, it's follow through.) Sure enough, we had a paper trail to prove our case. But did that make any difference? No, because I can't really bring that up. If I bring that up or begin to question the accountability on *their* side, it would look like I'm justifying something. It's never a good idea to argue with someone who has already made up his or her mind.

I could see that my client was in quicksand – and I was joining them! I had to stop spinning my wheels and realize *I* was stuck. At that point in time, there was no opportunity to make a difference for that client. And if I really looked at it, I had seen the symptoms long before they got upset.

If you feel like you're spinning your wheels, stop now and get present. It might not be so easy to admit. But if you embrace the fact that these symptoms are trying to tell you that you may be stuck, you are halfway home.

Symptoms of Unstuck

Oh, by the way, what does unstuck feel like? You feel like you're moving within the flow of life. Like there is wind beneath your wings. Just like the seagulls I love to watch when I'm in Dubrovnik, Croatia. I sit and watch the graceful creatures fly. They just go from one wind current to the next as they glide above the Adriatic Sea, fully present to the hunt, the wind, and their environment. There is no resistance; just their wings spreading, taking life as it lifts them higher. For me, that's what unstuck feels like.

Instead of worry or anxiety, you feel a sense of power – power to take those actions you know you need to take in each moment, or to get the resources that you need, or to get yourself sorted out so you're in the right mindset to really fulfill on what you want to fulfill on. You know you're unstuck when obstacles really seem more like challenges or opportunities. They are just new currents of air that take your game to the next level. They don't throw you off your game.

When you finally find yourself unstuck, you know that you are living your life to the fullest. Rather than being fixated on getting certain results, you are led by having a powerful vision that you have created. You don't let your history define your destiny and you don't let fears of an unknown future stop your forward motion. Unstuck is firing on all cylinders in your career, your relationships, and your spiritual/emotional/physical health. When you are in the flow of life, doing work that you love with real purpose, all of those emotions – the excitement, inspiration, and gratitude – will be present a vast majority of the time. They are the surest indicators that you are unstuck. It's good. Very good.

It's (Mostly) All in Your Head

But being stuck, both mentally and physically, can bring down any warrior. Sure, you've trained, you've learned the tactics. But when you finally hit that imaginary brick wall, you're fighting against an invisible enemy. As entrepreneurs, what we often don't realize is that the real source of the problem usually isn't in the "external" material issues, like not enough cash flow, untrained staff, or a limited market. Our stuckness is more often an internal issue: how you're using your mind and how you perceive what's going on. The "stuck" mindset is the most insidious issue someone can face, and it can be seriously debilitating to personal and professional progress. But in some ways, it is also the easiest to solve. This is because the source of the problem comes down to only one person— you.

The majority of this book will focus on those internal mindset issues. Having an issue with your mindset is akin to wearing invisible blinders: You are getting lots of data, so you believe that you can see what's happening. But the truth is, you aren't getting the whole picture. Anyone who knows anything about horses can tell you that whatever they think they see is their operational reality. Nothing outside of those blinders exists. Maybe this makes sense for horses, but not so much for human beings trying to create or run a business. And although we may like to believe otherwise, the human mind tends to work as if we were wearing blinders, except that our blinders are perceptual rather than corporeal.

Here's the secret: ***Getting unstuck is all about awareness and being totally present in the moment.*** That's it. Nothing more. And if you and I could do those two things really well even 10% of the time, we wouldn't need the rest of this book! But most of us aren't fully present and aware even 1% of the time, and most of us relate more to the stuck symptoms than what it feels like to be unstuck. You don't notice that you're soaking in a hot pot with a bunch of naked hippies; it's just the way it is.

We get so wrapped up in this alternate reality of being stuck that we don't even notice what is around us. If we are lucky, every once in a while, we wake up for a moment and notice. Sometimes we are so asleep that we need a big alarm clock. Dubrovnik, Croatia, was that for me.

As I write this, my partner and I (and our dogs, Bailey and Brodee) are spending the winter in Croatia. When we set out on our adventure, we didn't know where in Croatia we were going to land. Now, I am a free spirit and love traveling and flying by the seat of my pants. And I don't even care if it's the only pair of pants I have; as long as I have my toothbrush, I am good to go.

At least that was my philosophy when I was younger and backpacked through Europe. Now that I'm a little older (alright, quite a bit older), what is important to me has changed. A toothbrush is definitely close to the top of the list, but now I also need high speed internet access and a pet-friendly place to stay.

Before we started out on our new adventure, I had picked out a couple of towns for us to check out to see if that was where we want to land for the winter. Right from the start I was a little crazed about finding the perfect apartment, in the perfect location, and – oh yeah –pet friendly with high-speed internet access. No small feat. The first stop was Split, an awesome city with its Palace of the Emperor Diocletian and Riviera along the

Adriatic. To say that it's amazing is an understatement. While the city is spectacular, the apartment we rented was the size of our closet in the U.S.—I wish I were joking about that. On the plus side, it did have a great bathroom.

But since we were not living in the bathroom, we only stayed there a couple of days until it was time to check out the next city on the list. I think George Bernard Shaw summed up Dubrovnik best by saying, "Those who seek paradise on Earth should come to Dubrovnik and see Dubrovnik." Apart from the Amalfi Coast in Italy, it's the most spectacular place I have ever seen. But I didn't pay much attention to where we were, truthfully. It was just like the hot water I was soaking in.

I was constantly thinking about the next city we planned to visit. I kept researching the different cities and apartments in those cities. Oh sure, every once in a while I got up and walked out to our balcony, which overlooked Dubrovnik and the Adriatic Sea. Really to just clear my head so I could get back to the work at hand: finding a perfect apartment (an apartment with a spectacular view), the perfect location (like paradise on Earth), and pet friendly. So leaving Bailey and Brodee hanging out on the balcony, happy as pigs in #$&!, I would head to my laptop to find the perfect place. Insane, right?

Everything I wanted was right under my nose. But, I was sleepwalking, hanging out in my head and not out in the world. Sometimes we are so asleep we don't even know that we're stuck. And the ironic thing is that if you just get present, you'd realize you are not stuck and everything you want is right under your nose. If you just stop and listen to the naked astrologer in the hot pot, it all turns out. I woke up and realized I was in Paradise.

So let's keep going.

PURPOSE

Our society is evolving, and it is clear to me the business paradigm is slowly shifting from profit to purpose. How do you, and your business, fit into that paradigm?

I was on a conference call not too long ago when a colleague shared some challenges he was facing. What was fascinating was that it could have been me talking. It was like he was sharing exactly what I had been experiencing. I just sat and listened while all the other people on the call gave him business advice – actually very good, insightful advice – about what he should be doing to resolve the challenges. But just like me, it was clear he didn't need more things to do. On all business measures, this guy was a success. He knew exactly what he needed to generate in order to make his business thrive and make as much money as he wanted to make. But unspoken between the lines, I could hear that he was actually starting to ask one of the big questions: "What is the purpose of my life?" In other words, he didn't want to know what to *do* but who he's supposed to *be*.

As the world is changing and the economy is uncertain, people are really searching for new ways to communicate and a new language to navigate these uncharted waters. In this amazing point in history, with the internet and its abundance of information at our fingertips and all the different opportunities available to us, I think many people are scared and confused. They don't really realize that we don't need to feel lost – that we're already fluent in the language that makes all these things happen. We've just forgotten it.

Stepping Back

You know that old Tina Turner song "What's Love Got to Do with It"? If you're too young to know what I'm talking about, go immediately and download this song. It's a classic. And if you're asking yourself, "What does he mean 'download'?", just keep reading. Now, why am I talking about love in a business book? Because love is the key to finding out if you're stuck on the spiritual level. I know these words aren't thrown around a lot in business books. But, I believe it's why so many entrepreneurs are stuck. They've quit listening to what their spirit wants. If the word spirit throws you, please replace it with whatever you call being connected to all of it. The jig is up. We are all connected; science has proven it. So now, instead of asking the question, "How does this serve me?", we need to ask ourselves, "How does this serve everyone?" (spirit).

In this chapter, I want you to forget whatever specific career quandary you're wrestling with and ask yourself honestly, "Is it my spirit that is stuck?" I know that question might have you say, "What?" But just hang out with it for a while. I think many of us get stuck on a spiritual level even though it appears we're stuck on little, annoying challenges in our lives or our careers. The truth is that those little annoying challenges simply melt away when we've tackled and answered the big questions. I've

seen it in my own life and in the lives of my clients over and

over again. Once you've discovered your purpose, your spirit's

calling – that direction that makes you eager to leap out of bed

in the morning —how to meet payroll, whether to update to

the latest technology, where your business should be located –

all the issues that made you feel stuck become opportunities to

fulfill your purpose.

The things that *truly* make a difference will solve the practical

issues that you are facing in your life and in your business. I

wrote this book with the intent of presenting solutions for

practical issues that people face in their lives and businesses—

to have people see the places where they are stuck, particularly

when it comes to starting, shifting, or expanding their work.

But this isn't a book about how to 'make money', because I've

never witnessed 'making money' as a life purpose that really

holds water or keeps us moving over the long run. And it's this

illusion that 'making money' to satisfy our every whim is going to make us happy. We buy into what advertisers and the media is selling . . . hook, line, and sinker. More toys make us happier. And if you are not happy, the next whatever-it-is will be the answer. *Then* you will be happy.

This belief leaves many people in the United States walking around numb, disconnected, zoned out. We are dependent on drugs – both legal and illegal – to treat our depression and malaise; our actual face time is waning as our Facebook time waxes. There is a major undercurrent of dissatisfaction. People are feeling disconnected from the planet, their families, their friends, and themselves. We have begun to seriously question whether the way we've been prioritizing our lives is good, and whether valuing material wealth and achievement over spiritual harmony has led us astray. We are beginning to sense that we are a species that needs more than just a steady paycheck to bring us real fulfillment.

As an entrepreneur or business owner yourself, you may have experienced this numbness. On conference calls these days, I notice more and more business leaders and entrepreneurs waking up and asking themselves, "What is this all for?" They are very successful by most measures and some make millions. They have the formula for success, but there's this fundamental uneasiness that something is missing. They say to themselves, "I have the house, the car, the lifestyle, and I am still not happy. What am I doing wrong?" They have a profound feeling that they have missed their path. At the end of the day, although they are making a difference and everything may look right on the outside, they feel stuck and unfulfilled.

The positive side here is that we are finally beginning to know we aren't happy. We aren't the car spinning its wheels, believing it is moving. We can finally see that we are incredibly stuck. We've become too miserable to ignore the situation anymore. We are yearning to regain that connection with our community, both the smaller community surrounding us and the human community at large, as well as that sense of being connected to ourselves. We want to feel a sense that all is right with the world. We want to feel passionate about life and what we are doing.

The idea of purpose has grown almost to be a legend, to the point where finding yours is like searching for the Holy Grail. It's become this long, arduous quest that leaves people feeling lost and helpless. But it isn't all for nothing. I agree with all the emphasis and energy surrounding finding your purpose in life. But I think the generation we live in today has developed some misconceptions around the idea. Just as we've been fooled by Hollywood into thinking we have a single soul mate, the perfect mate for whom we must search far and wide, we've also been sold into thinking that we have a single, highly important and big hairy deal purpose. With the insanely high divorce rate in the United States, the idea of "the one" has shattered; and I think it's about time we cracked the mystery of finding our purpose as well. We have been sold the notion there is a one and only purpose for each of us. A lot of us are confused, baffled, and bewildered; and it leaves us in inaction.

But I don't think it should be a search. Like when I was in Dubrovnik and realized everything I wanted was right under my nose, all you need to do is look up. It's with you, all the time, like the Northern Star. The Northern or North Star is the prominent star that lies closest in the sky to the north celestial pole. It's been used for centuries as a beacon, helping travelers find their way home.

Your North or Northern Star is your purpose always truing you up, always returning you to those things that are important, those things that really light you up and make you sing (even if it's not out loud). Whenever you're stuck or lost in life, your purpose is always going to be the thing that gets you back on track. You don't have to *find* it. You just have to look a little closer because it's always been there. The hard part isn't discovering your purpose, but living it. It takes a lifetime to truly explore and delve into who you are meant to *be*. And even though straying from the path is part of the journey, it doesn't mean we have to stray for long. As long as we have that

Northern Star, our purpose, we can always find the way back on course.

A Simple Statement

But I bet you're thinking, "Is it really all that simple?" It really is. In fact, you should be able to express your purpose in a single sentence. We have this romantic notion that it will take an entire novel to express something as important, as grand, as our purpose in life. But it's not a Shakespearean epic. It's a simple statement that captures your unique way of being and interacting with life. Let me repeat: Our purpose is simply a way of being and interacting with life. We chose to come here and play this game of life and I think we chose a mission that is about what we really want to explore and delve into during this lifetime.

Sometimes it is easier to see this in action with other people than ourselves. Take Harrison, my senior writer and editor at Wasabi Publicity, who worked for 22 years in the newspaper industry. He and I were chatting one day and I asked him about his purpose. "Purpose? What do you mean?" I said, "What is that thing that you love to do that gets you out of bed every morning? You know, that thing that has kept you in this industry all these years?" He thought about it for a second, then said, "I feel driven to find out everything I can about each news story, whether it's large or small."

It was no accident that Harrison's articles were frequently placed on the front page, were often picked up by news wires, and consistently won awards for enterprise and investigative reporting. When you are clear about your purpose, everything falls into place. But what was the source of this excellence? Simple: his purpose. "I discovered that what really motivated me was that I was always learning something new with each story I wrote," he says. "That sense of curiosity translated into my writing in a way that made people want to read my articles."

Harrison's simple purpose is to delve into his curiosity and learn. He now uses that curiosity to write press kits, articles, and pitches for our clients. His story illustrates how being tapped into your purpose can light you up and give you energy. When that happens, you're in the zone. That spark is how you feel when you have found and are living your purpose. It is those juices that get you unstuck – it's your expression, your passion, your calling. It doesn't feel like an accident that you are doing what you what you are doing. Following your purpose is your access to being in the flow and getting unstuck.

This doesn't have to be complicated. Really! Just look at what lights you up in life or ask people in your life, "What am I doing when I look the happiest?" They may give you a quizzical look, but just stick with the conversation. They know. Remember, we are all connected.

For me, it's simple. I am the happiest when I am being great with people. I love building rapport and being great and gracious with people. So it really doesn't really matter what I am *doing* as long as I can still fulfill that purpose. I am now the CEO of Wasabi Publicity, but I could be working in a Starbucks and still fulfill the purpose of being great with people and making a difference. Sometimes I've gone into Starbucks and had such amazing service it has really altered my whole day – which made a difference for me and allowed me to make a difference for other people. So I could fulfill my purpose of making a difference for people serving vente skinny caramel macchiatos as well!

The other piece to my purpose that lights me up is to have conversations. Not any conversations, but conversations that have people looking at the world in a different way. That gives them a new perspective, an 'Aha!' moment that gives them clarity to fulfill their purpose. I am so grateful that my clients allow me to make that contribution to them so *they* can change the world.

Being vs. Doing

This brings up an important point: Purpose is not about what you *do* but who you will *be*. I fundamentally believe we are each put on the planet for a specific purpose, but not necessarily to *do* a specific something. I think we were put on this planet to *be* something. People get themselves confused by trying to figure out what they should be *doing* before understanding who they are meant to *be*. I hear a lot of "What work am I supposed to *do*?" or "What good am I meant to *do* in this lifetime?" But the real question to answer is, "Who should I *be* on the planet?" or better yet, "Who am I really?"

Our western culture places a lot of emphasis and value on what we do and what we have (which is directly connected to what we do). People get so caught up in doing the doing so they can have the having that they completely miss the being! And for many of us, what we do and what we have defines us: "I'm a doctor." "I live in such and so neighborhood." But that's bass-ackwards. What you do doesn't define who you are. Who you *are* should define what you *do*; and from that, what you *have* flows naturally. When you know who you are meant to be, the actions you should take to give you access to what you really want become quite clear. But the opposite rarely brings a sense of fulfillment.

Landing that great job and working 80 hours a week to get all the material trappings just isn't what it's all about. If you check in with some of the most successful, wealthiest people in the world, they'll tell you the truth. The ones who approached life backwards find out that the American Dream of landing a great job and getting the car/house/toys/stuff won't make you happy. These people end up feeling bankrupt and profoundly unhappy, and they'll often admit it. But the successful, wealthy people who approached life forwards—coming from who they really are to do what they do in the world – will tell you that they would still be happy being and doing what they've done even if they didn't get paid for it! It's not that you can't be wealthy and know your purpose, but wealth shouldn't be confused with your purpose. So, you shouldn't feel like you're earning your purpose, but rather whatever you're doing should fulfill the person you are being.

Most of us don't get much support for sitting around thinking "Who should I be in the world?" We're entrepreneurs, for gosh sake, and we've got our businesses to run! But if we keep running on that hamster wheel without asking that very essential question – Who am I meant to be?—how does that work out for us?

When we don't know our purpose and who we are meant to be, we end up living our lives as we've been programmed. It's more like playing a game (someone else's game!) versus living life. When we start from the *doing* and *having*, everything becomes superficial to the point that what's really important to you gets tossed out the window. It's not as if you don't have ambitions and goals, but they've probably been pushed to the back of your mind, or confused with those superficial goals. And it feels crummy.

It's About Happiness

A key to who you are meant to be and your purpose is your happiness. What makes you happy? Deeply and satisfyingly happy? I don't mean the kind of happy that lasts for a nanosecond. Maybe you're happy when your team wins the playoff or you lose that extra 10 pounds or you find the perfect parking spot. You might be happy when you get a new car or are invited to a terrific party. But how long does that kind of happy last? That's more like the Chinese food kind of happy – you're hungry again 20 minutes later! Your team loses its next game or those 10 pounds come back; the new car needs oil changes and the party's over. But there's another kind of happy. It's where you feel like you're in the flow of who you are meant to be.

For example, my business partner Michelle is happiest when she is teaching. Whether it's giving someone media training or showing someone the basics of whitewater rafting, she is thrilled that she can share knowledge with someone and coach them. She'll go into teaching mode no matter what. When she is being a teacher or mentor in any kind of situation, she feels happy and fulfilled. Could she have chosen a bunch of different things to *do* as a teacher? Sure. And probably she could find happiness and fulfillment in a variety of careers as long as she could be who she really is, a teacher.

I don't think this kind of happiness should be taken lightly. Without it, we start acting like robots: cold and unfeeling, operating by rote, uninspired – and we need to start living again. So ask yourself, "Who should I be *being*?" What are those things that really light you up and turn you on? A lot of us could say, "But there are a lot of those things!" That's great. But if you really boil it down and look, they probably all have a similar essence or theme to them, and within that essence or theme is your purpose.

What's Important

I like to make a distinction between 'what's important to you' and 'your purpose'. There are many things that are important to you now and also things that are important as you change and go forward through your life, but your purpose won't change. For example, if you become a father, being with your

43

kids and mentoring them and protecting them will undoubtedly be significantly important to you. Little League games and ballet recitals, paying the orthodontist and saving for college funds, figuring out the balance between keeping them safe and giving them freedom — during the early parenting years, these things will be important while other things (maybe travel, adventure, and sleep!) will take a back seat. You care about different things at that time than you did when you were single, and it will change again when the kids are grown and off creating lives of their own. But if you look to see the essence of your life's purpose during these different phases, it remains pretty much the same.

The trap is that people think things that are important to them are their life's purpose, but they are not. For instance, the parent example: If you mistakenly think that your life's purpose is to raise your children, what happens after they grow up and leave the nest? Empty nesters' syndrome, right? But if you understand that this level of parenting is not your life purpose but something that is important to you during a certain time, it won't throw you off as much. Your purpose will continue to be your North Star as you find different things that become important to you.

But that doesn't mean that knowing what is important to you is something you should disregard either. What's important to you is still important! Even though what is important to you is constantly changing, it's these kinds of things that keep you level headed and feeling fresh. What's important to you will keep you from digging a deeper hole when you're feeling stuck. And those things that are important to you will help define the way in which you express your purpose.

Take me for example. Being a global citizen and travel are important to me. Having money to live a certain lifestyle and having the freedom to work from anywhere in the world are important to me. For me, my purpose is really being great with people. If nothing else mattered, I could be working at a Starbucks, being great with people, and still be fulfilling my purpose. Wouldn't that be easy? But it wouldn't get me to the things that are important to me. Being CEO of Wasabi allows me to both fulfill on my purpose and pursue those things that are important to me. But if I mistook travel as my purpose, I might have ended up just moving to Budapest to immerse myself in the culture and finding any old type of job to support myself. I'm pretty sure that it wouldn't take long for me to feel dissatisfied, like something was missing from my life. Instead, I've taken the work that fulfills on my purpose (public relations with Wasabi) and figured out a way to expand it into Europe so – voila! – I get to live part-time in Budapest after all!

Your purpose will always be that overarching essence through your life. The trick is to find your purpose and then do those things that are important to you. Once you discover your purpose, the things you find important will naturally flow through it. And if you still aren't sure what your purpose is, knowing what's important to you can be a jump start.

Things that are important to you don't always have to be things you've already done. Maybe you've been thinking about doing something for the longest time, but never got around to doing it. I've always thought I'd love to travel, but it was really only at the age of 30 that I got around to truly exploring this passion of mine. When I finally found the opportunity, I went on an escapade and stole away to Europe for the summer. Coming back, I felt totally invigorated and gained a completely new perspective of the world and a way of living. That would be only the very beginning of my adventures in Europe and would be a big turning point for what I saw as important to me and how it would tie in with my purpose.

And that's the feeling I'm talking about, feeling alive and gaining perspective. Once you gain that inspiration, you start wanting to take action. So think about it, your priorities will change as you grow, but it'll help you see life in a different light. Once you start to look at the essence of your life, you'll start to see a path. Follow that path and you'll find yourself being guided by your Northern Star.

Nailing It Down

Maybe at this point in your life you haven't pinpointed your purpose, uncovered that simple statement of who you are meant to be. Not a problem! I don't believe that we have one sole purpose on this earth, so discovering it shouldn't be like searching for a needle in a haystack. Rather, it should be something familiar and comfortable. Some people think that your purpose comes to you in some form of epiphany. But I think it's the essence of all the things that are most important to you, that make you happy. It's that feeling you get when you've felt in rhythm with the universe. Not many things can give us that same satisfaction, so you shouldn't have to look too far to find your purpose. Or maybe the problem isn't that you haven't uncovered your purpose, but that you haven't made it a priority in your life – yet! Either way, let's get down to business. And look up to the Northern Star.

What's Important Exercise

What I have found life changing has been my practice in meditation. I know, it seems silly – sitting crossed-legged and focusing on your breath – but in all actuality, it gives you a higher sense of being. You don't have to go all hippy-style. But I suggest you give contemplation a shot as a vehicle to uncover what's important to you and your purpose. Simply go to your favorite place. That doesn't mean you have to fly to Paris, but it could be as simple as sitting in your favorite comfy chair or going to that one coffee shop you love. Any place that makes you feel at peace and clear headed. By being in your comfy place, you're priming yourself to start thinking about your life. Now go back through your life and think about the things that have made you the happiest. Think of those defining moments where you just came out feeling

that everything was right in the world. You might be surprised by what comes up. Some of those times may be grand and significant. Others may seem like small, simple events. Accept whatever comes to you.

Next, either on your laptop or on a pad of paper, depending on your preference, start to list all those things that are most important to you and really be thorough about it. While thinking, there are probably a lot of things that have changed over the years, as life usually does. What you're looking for among all these important things are those that have remained consistent, that you love to do, and that have made you the happiest. You'll start to notice a pattern about the things that have remained important to you over time. Begin to narrow that list down to the top things that are *most* important to you.

What next? Well, you've realized what *has* been important to you– now think of what is important to you at this very moment. This will allow things that are important to you to align from past to present. Now looking at everything on your list, what exactly about them made you happy? Were you spreading great ideas or bringing people together? Were you challenging yourself or expressing light and laughter? Who were you *being* during those times?

Next, take a break. An exhaustive list is called exhaustive for a reason! Give yourself a few minutes or a few days before coming back to your list. With fresh eyes, look again at your list and the reasons those activities or events made you happy. What do they have in common? What are the common themes? These common themes are pointing toward your purpose. And what will begin to emerge are things you would love *doing* while fulfilling your purpose as a way of *being*. Don't ignore those things that are important to you because they give your life juice, inspiration, and rejuvenation when you need it. Make sure they don't get lost under your endless To-Do lists!

It's really that simple. It might seem like an epiphany, but really it's just a moment of clarity, an 'aha' moment where everything just makes sense.

Values

The core values you hold in life are also connected to your purpose but are not your purpose itself. Your core values can lead you to your purpose and help define how you express your purpose in the same way that the things that are important to you can. So what are values exactly? Your core values will be characteristics like honesty, integrity, beauty, grace, kindness, excellence, courage, humor, or harmony. It's those qualities that you appreciate in others and you hope to express in your own life. When you are not expressing your core values in different areas of your life, you feel as one of my clients put it, "uncomfortable in your own skin." You feel dissatisfied and usually find yourself stuck.

For example, say that innovation and creativity are two of your core values. If you find yourself in a job or a relationship that is more about maintenance than innovation, you may feel restless and out of sorts. Or say that you value face-to-face human connection. You may find that spending time texting or on Facebook and LinkedIn feels hollow and not satisfying, even if it's getting you some of the results you may be looking for.

But pinpointing your core values, in conjunction with identifying your purpose, can give you clear direction and help you sort through the many options (sometimes too many options!) life offers. For instance, if you recognize that you value innovation, you may not want to choose a partner who is resistant to risk and change. You may want to consider businesses and careers that force you to stay on the cutting edge while you fulfill your purpose. If you value face-to-face interaction, you may choose to attend networking events as opposed to beefing up your social media campaign.

In my personal case, one of my core values is being gracious with people. So within my purpose of 'being great with people' and helping them succeed, I feel most aligned with who I really am when I do it graciously. I could never be one of those coaches who yells and bullies his athletes or the investment broker who only gives clients nanoseconds of his time. I want to spend quality time with my clients, lead them gently to what they need to know, and help them feel great about themselves in the process. If I didn't fulfill my purpose this way, I would feel off track no matter how well I was doing. So it's helpful to identify your core values so you can throw them into the mix as you make decisions about your career and your life.

Core Values Exercise

Let's approach values in the same way we identified what's important to us. Go to your comfy place where you feel at peace and free to muse.

Take the following list along with you as a starting point:

autonomy	beauty	caring	challenge
courage	creativity	dignity	elegance
excellence	excitement	fairness	freedom
fulfillment	fun	grace	happiness
abundance	power	kindness	respect
family	humility	education	bliss
harmony	helping	honesty	humor
innovation	joy	justice	learning
love	mastery	order	perseverance
playfulness	revolution	safety	security
self-actualization	self-reliance	service	simplicity
problem solving	creating change	synergy	truth
uniqueness	vitality	wisdom	zest

Pick values from this list and think of others by asking, "What qualities, if they were missing in my life, would make me feel less authentic, less alive, or less like my true self?" When you have an exhaustive list, start to winnow it down. If you could only have ten of those values in your life, which are most important to you? What if you could only have three? If possible, prioritize your values into the categories of "Must Have," "Nice to Have," and "I'm Really Okay Without It."

Going forward, know that your "Must Haves" should be incorporated into all areas of your life. Without them, you'll never feel right with the world. Your "Nice to Haves" will add additional joy and satisfaction to your life. And your "I'm Really Okay Without It" categories can be ignored for the most part, because we only have so much energy in life. Shouldn't we focus it on the qualities we truly value? For example, I know my values truly are a testament for what I chose to do as a career. Making a difference and helping others make a difference are probably my biggest priorities. I also highly value having a flexible work schedule, like working whenever and wherever works for both my clients and me. And like most anybody, I also value making good money in order to fund my other passions in life, like traveling. Being the CEO of Wasabi, I've been able to keep true to myself and what I value and that's why I am so comfortable in my own skin. So, once you've prioritized your top ten, you can start to really see and evaluate your opportunities.

To help you uncover your purpose if you've not already identified it, glance at your top ten values. How do you like to express them? Is it in relationship to people, things, ideas? How do these values show up in your personal and professional life? Can you sense a theme that reflects your purpose?

Your Company's Purpose

Now let's apply all of this to your business. How does your current business fit with your purpose, your values, and what's important to you? Keep in mind that your business is just a vehicle. Your purpose, values, and what's important can be fulfilled in several different vehicles. Both the hybrid and the SUV are going to get you where you want to go. The question is, which one is going to make the drive most enlivening for YOU? For example, what if your purpose is to teach spiritual principles? You could fulfill on that purpose by teaching martial arts or being an executive coach or having your own TV show or your OWN network – or being a minister! What if your purpose is to bring joy to others? You could be a humorous writer or make exquisite chocolates or offer hot air balloon rides. See what I mean?

In a perfect world, you would determine what your business would be *after* you're clear on your purpose, values, and things that are important. One of the stories I love is how Paula Deen decided on her business. She had a phobia, agoraphobia. She wouldn't go out in public and she was a single mother. I watched an interview with her and she said that the kitchen was where she could really lose herself. Cooking isn't just her skill, it's her passion. Someone looking at her would say she is just throwing food together, but it is really a way of being to her. And notice how she was able to parlay her passion into a huge empire. She did it based on the essence of her purpose. And even though her values changed over time from southern comfort cooking to health eating, her North Star remains constant.

But since most of us aren't taught to choose our careers based on our life's purpose, you may have chosen yours based on something else (i.e. what business will make me the most money?) For some of us, it's a little harder to read the writing on the wall than others. (I'm not mentioning any names.)

It wasn't until *after* I started Wasabi Publicity and looked back on my life and the decisions I made, that things started to fall into place. All the pieces fit beautifully.

Believe it or not, I have a degree in chemical engineering. I know – crazy, right? What was I thinking? No offense to all you engineers out there, but I think even my professors knew I wasn't a fit. It was like that Sesame Street song about shapes.

They show four shapes: three of which are circles and one lonesome square. It's clear that the square doesn't belong there, but they rub it in by singing a little ditty –"One of these things is not like the others, one of these things just doesn't belong . . ." – and that pretty much sums up 'me in engineering school'. Don't get me wrong, I wasn't a square; I had spiky hair, a pierced ear, and ripped jeans; but I did stick out like a sore thumb. It was pretty clear being a chemical engineer was not 'it' for me.

So why did I pick that in the first place? Good question. It was all Mrs. Yaney's fault, my high school chemistry teacher. I loved chemistry class! (Don't say anything). So one day, in a moment of clarity, I walked up to Mrs. Yaney to share my newly discovered passion to let her know I was thinking of pursuing chemistry as a career. I was a little shocked when she replied, "You don't want to become a chemist, Drew. It's boring and you won't make any money. What you want to do is become a chemical engineer. That's the highest paid BS (Bachelor of Science, not the other kind) out there."

I was sold. Visions of BMWs began dancing in my head.

Off I went to college to make my visions a reality. During my eight years at school (yes, eight! I was a junkie), I took everything from math and physics, to ballet and economics. You name it, I took it. I loved being in school – it rekindled my passion to make a difference – but it didn't take long for me to realize the *vehicle* to get me where I wanted to go was not chemical engineering. So I left college with a degree and an insight that money was not the highest priority for me.

Actually, I knew I wanted to make a difference from the time I was 15 years old. Of course, I had no idea how my life was going to unfold to make that happen. But I'll never forget sitting in the ballroom of Hotel Utah underneath magnificent crystal chandeliers when I discovered my true passion in life. Hotel Utah sits right across the street from the Salt Lake LDS

(Mormon) Temple, the corner stone of downtown Salt Lake City.

An appropriate place to fine one's passion in life, right?

Now, I'm not saying that sitting on a hard chair in a 100-year-old hotel, no matter how beautiful, is the way for you to find your true calling. But it was for me. It was there during an Erhard Seminars Training *est* Course, that I saw the power of having a conversation. Not just any conversation, though. A conversation for possibility.

In that room, I was fascinated how these (seemingly) 'put together' adults were talking about what was going on in their lives. "OMG, adults are a mess!" I thought to myself. It was right there and then I decided that when I was an adult I was not going to screw up my life.

Oh the joys of being 15 and naïve!

But along with the screwed up adults, there were other people present: trainers – amazing transformation trainers. Those trainers were so miraculous that I also decided that whatever they were doing, I wanted to do that too. Conversation, that's all it was. But during those conversations, those screwed up adults seemed to have their lives shift on a dime. You could physically see it on their faces. There was freedom in their lives that hadn't seen the light of day for a long, long time. I was hooked and clear about what *I* wanted to do: give people *that* kind of freedom.

Sometimes after you have those bursts of clarity in life you back it up with actions, and sometimes you don't. I didn't. After completing that intense course that changed my life (and the lives of many others), I headed back to the 'real world' at Layton High School. At least, it was *my* real world: a world full of chemistry and BMWs pulling me away from my calling.

After my slight college detour of eight years, I was back on track, clear about the difference I wanted to make. So I went to work for Landmark. (If you don't know about Landmark, check them out at www.LandmarkWorldwide.com) A fundamental principle of Landmark's work is that people – and the communities, organizations, and institutions with which they are engaged – have the possibility not only of success, but also of fulfillment and greatness. Working at Landmark was a true pleasure. Today, I never have to ask myself if my life matters because, after working at Landmark, I know the answer to that question. And I cannot express how grateful I am that Wasabi gets to be the publicity company that represents them.

Have you ever noticed how things in life come to full circle? I was working for Landmark and leading their programs when I met my current business partner, Michelle Tennant Nicholson. Michelle was one of THOSE students. Let's just say, type A personality. She would stand up in her overalls, Doc Martins, and pigtails and challenge everything I said. She was going to get her money's worth. It makes me laugh to think back and ask myself, "How did this all happen?"

At the age of thirty, I was bitten by travel bug. I wanted to see the world, so I packed up my stuff and headed to Europe. I could write a whole book on *that* adventure, but that would be more of an *Eat, Pray, Love* finding oneself kind of book (which for sure is a way to get unstuck. If your bags *are* packed, don't forget to include this book! You never know, you might find yourself stuck in Rome. But if you don't have your bags packed for Europe, let's continue *this* journey.)

Fast forward 10 years.

Michelle and I were hanging out as friends and I turned to her and said, "Hey, we should go into business together!" She said, "Doing what?" And I said, "I don't know, we'll figure that out." We were in Ohio at the time and I said, "Oh, and by the way, I'm moving to Asheville, North Carolina. Why don't you move with me?" Michelle, being a risk taker and kayaker, was more than happy to pack up and move to the whitewater kingdom of Asheville.

So it was settled. We were moving to a new location together and starting a new business. But before we could move into the house I bought, there were a few repairs that needed to be done. Meaning, everything.

So we were traveling back and forth from Ohio to Asheville and it was on one of those six-hour road trips that I began sharing with Michelle what I really wanted to do with my life. I wanted to create a company that got up underneath those people who were committed to making a difference and support them in making that difference. Michelle said, "That's PR!" Michelle's background was PR and, as she began to distinguish PR for me, everything fell into place.

It was *that* conversation that sparked Wasabi Publicity. All the pieces of the puzzle fit: making a difference, being great with people, and making money so I could be free to do the things I love to do.

If you see your business doesn't provide all the pieces the puzzle, well, you may need to regroup and choose differently. Don't make this too complicated; don't throw the baby out with the bath water. Often the business you have can fulfill your purpose with a few adjustments. Are you a physical therapist whose purpose is to entertain people? Great! Is there a way you can be entertaining while you work with your clients' aches and pains? Or maybe your purpose is to build bridges between people but your business is computer programming. Can you become that person who helps non-techies understand techies (and vice versa) so they can create brilliant applications together? Wasabi was the whole enchilada for me. I get the privilege to fulfill my purpose and relish those things in my life that are important to me.

Day to Day Decisions

By uncovering your purpose, values, and what's important to you, you have access to a foundation from which you can look to determine what actions to take. As entrepreneurs, as I know too well myself, we have zillions of opportunities and possibilities coming at us. It can be overwhelming and leads to being stuck in the sand. But with a strong foundation, you'll rarely run into the quicksand. From that foundation, you really can look to see and evaluate the opportunities that are coming down the pike. You're clear where to put your energy to work because you're moving toward those things that are most valuable to you. This is essential if you're an entrepreneur or are starting your own business because it keeps you from wandering off the path and determines your focus. Should you focus on your website? Facebook? Twitter? LinkedIn? Contacting people? Should you go to networking events? For all of those decisions, you can look through the filter of your foundation to choose which opportunity to pursue or not pursue.

Your purpose and values will guide you in even the smallest of decisions. How to set up your waiting room? If your purpose is to entertain, maybe a DVD player with funny clips and movies? If you value beauty, maybe fresh flowers? If adventure is important to you, maybe you have magazines about travel or rock climbing. With this foundation, you'll be clearer on how to market, what clients to target, what hours you want to work.

Without this foundation, how do you really make decisions?

Many of us get stuck trying to base our decisions solely on

what experts say, the latest trend (which disappears the

moment we recognize it!), or what others in our same

profession do. That external input is okay. But it's the internal

foundation that will make our decisions feel right and keep us

heading in a direction that really makes us happy.

Sticky Notes Exercise

Hopefully by now it's

becoming clear that

knowing your values,

purpose, and what's

important to you will

affect all areas of your life, including your career. At the

beginning of this chapter, I asked you to forget about whatever

business issue seemed to have you stuck. I still want to stay

"big picture" as you figure out what you value most with

regards to your business. Don't try to minimize yourself. Never settle for anything less than exactly want you want. So reach for your North Star (purpose) values and what's important to you, no matter how outlandish and out of reach these things may seem.

For this exercise, we'll use sticky notes and a big blank wall. What better way to express yourself and visualize the foundation of your business than with sticky notes! Sticky notes are always fun – they come in all sorts of colors and sizes, and sometimes can be a pain to keep organized; but the fact is that you can never have too many of them.

On each sticky note, write down things that are important to you in both your business and your personal life. Slap them all up on the wall. Next, write down your core values and how they might show up in your business. Put them up on the wall as well. Finally, write down a statement of your purpose and another statement about the purpose of your business. Stick these sticky notes up with the rest. Anything that matters to you in your life and business, write it down on a sticky note and plant it on your blank wall. Until you've totally drained your brain of all that is important to you, keep pulling those stickies! By the end of this, you should have a nice collage of sticky notes to observe and contemplate.

You'll notice, while doing this, that the things you considered important to your career ten years ago are not necessarily going to be what is most important to you now. For example, I know when we were starting out ten years ago, I felt it was important to build a great reputation in the U.S. Now, with that reputation built, I am focused on different things, like helping our clients make a difference globally. What's important may change over time, but your purpose and values probably won't.

When you have a wall full of sticky notes, step back and take it all in. Once you've cleared your head, take a look at your masterpiece and start to consider which ones truly are fundamentally important to you. What do you see? Does your business today reflect what shows up on that wall? What about particular decisions you've made or are trying to make? If you have people working for you, how do they fit into the mix? (At Wasabi, one of our practices is to identify the strengths, values, and purpose of our individual employees to make sure they are in positions most suited to them where they can really thrive and make their best contribution to the overall effort.) You may see that how you're running your business isn't a problem, but that you've lost focus on what you're committed to do as a result of your business.

Mission for Your Business

Imagine this: you walk into a Starbucks, place your order, and every possible things goes wrong: The server was rude, they give you the wrong drink, there's no more creamer in the canister, and they even misspell your name on the cup. You, the customer, are obviously frustrated and this experience taints your view of all other Starbucks. You might love your café latte but after that experience, you're willing to go find one somewhere else.

Starbucks has always been known for their happy-go-lucky service. If that standard isn't met in one store, the entire brand gets tainted as unsatisfactory. As customers, we expect the best experience and don't always consider the other side of the story. We don't know (or really care) if the barista is having a bad hair day or the manager had car trouble on the way to work. But that's how it's supposed to be because a business is meant to serve the customer.

So look at your business. When you feel stuck, you start to feel the heat. Once you start to lose sight of what your mission is, your focus falls more on YOU rather than the customer. But don't let it compromise what is important to you and the service you provide. If you find that you're more concerned about each day's cash flow or how much you've been working lately, then you're going to start feeling unhappy and you probably won't get the results you originally wanted. What you need to do at this point is just to stop and reconsider what you're committed to. You've become more focused on the logistics of everything than why you started your business. It's here that you're dishing out bad service and your customers are getting frustrated. There's no point in both of you losing out because of it.

So step back and find the source of your frustration. What got you to start your business in the first place? What are you trying to achieve? I know that my main goal at Wasabi is to help others be able to make a difference in the world. If I became more concerned with the amount of money I was making with each client, I would be betraying my own values. It might be that you have to stick to your guns and find your way back to your original calling, or that you have to reevaluate your game plan and change things up. When it comes down to it all, the customer should always come first, even if it means getting their coffee right.

So from the sticky notes on your wall, it's time to create a mission statement that will guide you through those down times and make your up times even more juicy. A mission statement doesn't have to be grand and fancy. It should speak to you and inspire you as well as anyone working with/for you. A mission statement might inspire or impress people outside of the company, but that's not really its purpose. It's meant for you, to keep your business on track. Here's an example of the mission statement we use for Wasabi:

Wasabi Publicity lives to launch conversations that make a difference and change the world.

It is not about us. The emphasis is on our clients and the service we provide for them. The more you focus on your clients and less on you, the happier all of you are going to be. Your mission is your unique expression that takes your purpose, values, and those things that are important to you and weaves it into a statement that expresses who you are, what you stand for, and what the world can count on from you.

Getting Unstuck Exercise

So you've taken the time to lay out your

values, the things that are important to

you, and to uncover your purpose. Yet

you still may find yourself getting stuck

in a particular area of life (health,

relationships, career, spiritual, financial). If so, it helps to re-

run the prior exercises with that specific area in mind. You

might find that your values or some of the things that are

important to you in one area of life are at cross-purposes with

what's important in another area. For example, you may value

producing exceptional results at work yet also feel it's

important to spend lots of quality time with your children. Is

the way you've set yourself up causing those two things to be

in conflict? Is there another way to produce exceptional results

that allows you to honor time with your kids?

So focus on that specific area of life that feels stuck. Jot down

all of your core values and what's important to you in that

specific area on your sticky notes and slap them up on the wall. Now step back. Which of those values are you not living? Which of the important things have you been ignoring or finding difficult to incorporate? When you've identified what might be missing, check and see if that value or important thing is in seeming conflict with the values and important things in another area of your life.

Next, get creative and 'negotiate' to achieve a win-win in both areas. Our common fallback position is to 'compromise' — meaning that one area of life gets the short stick or that both areas get less than they deserve. But assume there is a way to honor what's important in all areas of your life. What are the possibilities for doing that? This is the time to think out of the box, beyond the models you've always seen around you.

In this exercise, many of us notice that 'career' is the area that tends to suck our time and energy out of other areas of life. But the commitments we have beyond work are important too. One of my biggest passions is animals and Michelle shares this passion. Knowing that, we try to find ways to make it a priority in our lives. For example, we did a fundraiser at the time of Prince William and Kate Middleton's wedding. I knew I wanted to participate in this special moment in history, so Michelle and I staged a mock royal wedding —between our dogs! We set it up as a local fundraiser, so people made donations in lieu of gifts. It was such an amazing event that it created a shift in energy within the whole community. The event was a huge success and it felt awesome to get everyone to participate: the bakery donated a wedding cake, and the media even covered the event and caused quite a buzz.

So, not only did it make us feel good, the event showcased our community and the fact that Wasabi is committed to making a difference. Not only were we benefitting the community, but we became known in the community as a company that makes a difference. It's amazing when you're clear how everyone lines up to give you exactly what you want. It was an easy decision when considering this opportunity. We took two things that were important to us and made them work together

dynamically. This actually is great for entrepreneurs. Those

kinds of random acts of self-expression help you to become

known in your community as who you are and really what

you're committed to.

MIND TRAPS

One of our biggest assets can also be the thing that trips us up and gets us stuck: our minds. Used properly, our minds are the brilliant engines of creativity, productivity, and life satisfaction. Used improperly (which all of us do from time to time), our minds can become quicksand, a hamster wheel, or a lead-lined jail cell. Not good. So if you're feeling stuck, it may be because you aren't using your genius mind in the way it is intended. I call these mind traps.

One Thought Trap

Getting stuck in one (usually negative or unproductive) thought is one of the primary mind traps that causes people to get stuck. In general, anytime you are dominated by one thought over and over again, you are as stuck as stuck can be. It is very easy to let that kind of repetitive, fixated, circular brain noise dominate your world and your life. For some, it might be the fear of failure; in another, it could be concerns about physical or emotional safety. Or maybe you just can't let go of an event from the past, second-guessing choices you made weeks, months, or even years ago. Maybe you're even stuck in what looks like a "positive" thought. For example, you may be focused so narrowly on a goal that you're missing all of the opportunities that are showing up around you. Whatever the case may be, letting go of repetitive thinking, especially repetitive negative or narrow thinking, is central to moving your mindset into a better place.

Instinct

We are all born with survival instincts, some of which just boil down to common sense, right? Come out of the rain, look both ways before crossing, take a deep breath. But sometimes in the heat of some situation or other, we completely forget to use that instinct. We're so busy being clever and analytical and creative that we forget to say, "Hey! Does this even make sense?" But one of the most effective tools you can use when you're trying to get out of a difficult situation is your common sense. It seems silly, but sometimes people forget to use it in the most practical situations. To be successful and stay unstuck, we really have to develop a well-trained, commonsense, instinctual form of thinking. An experience of mine a few years back really woke me up to this fact and might spark some feelings of familiarity with your own experiences:

Michelle and I had been in business together for around six years and we were doing great. But despite Wasabi's success, I knew there was still something missing. At the start, Michelle and I had decided that Wasabi would be a boutique PR company because we are committed to working intimately with clients to ensure their success in the world. This felt great, but there was an entire market that we weren't able to serve under this model. So we decided to create a training program and market ourselves on the internet. We consulted some of the best internet marketers in the world and they told us exactly how to go about it. We did what they told us and started modeling them. We spent an incredible amount of energy putting the program together and launching our internet product. But while we were in the process of implementing this new campaign, something just didn't feel quite right. Looking back on it all, I didn't pay much attention to what we were being told to do by our consultants. I just followed their instructions with no second thoughts. I didn't bother to consult my own common sense and instinct. Heck, these guys were experts!

So let me cut to the chase. We launched the program and we were expecting to have a 100 people in the course – we got 12. The 12 people in the course got amazing results and, by the end, they were doing PR as well as any other publicist out there. This got us scratching our heads. We knew the product was high quality, but we didn't know how the heck to communicate that – which seems pretty strange for a PR company that specializes in communication, right? We continued to follow the advice of the experts and kept hitting our heads against a wall. After working on this project for six years, a light bulb went off: we needed to find our own unique expression. The thing that wasn't aligned was that it didn't fit our value to personally work with people. Not just to teach them, but mentor them – not from the stands, but out on the court. The field. That's what made the difference for our students and why they got great results. Now we don't focus on our internet training program. We simply mentor people, one-on-one, who want to learn the art of PR. Looking back, if I had only been paying attention to the signs, if I had used my common sense and instincts, we wouldn't have wasted all that time and energy. We could have made a bigger difference in the world by simply paying more attention.

Our school systems and our advanced training emphasize our left side analytical brain. We get trapped in being more and more clever in our thinking and strategizing. But sometimes we really need to rely more on our other instincts, to be more in tune to uncover and reveal what's really going on. It's our access to getting unstuck. It's about using our simple, common sense rather than our fancy schmancy cleverness.

Reaction vs. Proaction

Life is about being the hammer that hits the knee, not the spontaneous jerk afterwards.

The best offense is a good defense? Maybe. Life catches us by surprise sometimes and we do need to react. But we have more control over what happens than we give ourselves credit. What we need to figure out is, "Where in our 'life's vehicle' have we been the driver and where have we been the passenger?" As you start to think about this, know that being a passenger isn't a bad thing. In business, you need to know when to lead and when to listen. Maybe, as the passenger, you were the one holding the map and giving directions. The person driving may know the roads better than you do and by acknowledging that, you're going to get to your destination faster.

What you don't want to happen is to get booted to the back seat, even though it's your car! At that point, you shouldn't settle for going along for the ride, but put Billy into his place and reclaim the wheel. "Billy" in this analogy could be a number of things: the economy, that team of high-powered consultants you hired, even your staff. As an entrepreneur and business owner, you need to be in control of the steering wheel, even if you've hired a chauffeur to do the actual driving.

Another way of not being proactive could be that you're in the driver's seat but you've turned on the cruise control. Sure, there are times where it can make a long drive easier, but you lose a sense of urgency. It's at that point where life catches you off guard and you get into an accident. When you get too accustomed to operating on autopilot, you get used to only *observing* results rather than *producing* them. If this is the case, stop watching your life and business and start being active again! Maybe it's about time you turned your car around and found a different route, or you might end up in the sand.

To figure out if you've been taking action or taking the back seat, think about what actions you've been currently taking. Are they proactive or reactive? Is something or someone else "causing" you to act in a certain way or are you determining your own actions? If you're on the reactive side, you're quite likely to feel stuck. The quicksand has you and all you can do is flail around in reaction to it. But even if you find that you've been the one causing the action, you also have to think about whom you're acting for. Are your fulfilling your own agenda or someone else's? Your business shouldn't feel like a high school group project, where you end up doing all the work and the others just slap their name onto it. You started a business for a reason, because *you* had a mission. It's important to have a team and to know when to collaborate with others, but make sure that you're carrying out *your* role and achieving *your* goals.

For example, a colleague of mine was definitely struggling with feeling stuck. I was on a conference call and this guy was sharing some of the challenges he was facing. It was interesting to me because I really look up to this guy. For me, he's a guy who has completely figured it out. He is an expert in internet marketing and coaches entrepreneurs to achieve amazing business results and to get what they want out of life. All the other people on the call were giving him advice and sharing from their perspective on all the things that he should be doing. I listened carefully and realized that he had something else that needed to be addressed. For sure the answer wasn't for him to *do* more things. This guy is a master of his field and he knows exactly what he needs to do to generate as much money as he wants. But I could hear that he was actually struggling with the question of "What's the purpose of my life?" What he really needed to do was to close off his mind and stop thinking so much. He needed to start feeling more and listening to his instincts. It wasn't about doing more and being more clever in his thinking. The answer – which I believe he would easily know instinctually – was in doing less and doing what fulfills his commitments.

I think he senses as I do that the world is changing and the way business will be done is changing. It's becoming more and more about relationships. I heard someone say that relationships are the new currency, and I really do believe that. I think my colleague knew instinctively that was the direction that he needs to go to really fulfill his purpose in life. But he was so caught on his mind trap and figuring out new, improved things to do that he made himself stuck.

Over-thinking

Accessing your instinctual thinking doesn't mean you should never think and strategize.

It's an important ingredient in success. The problem comes in when we add too much of this ingredient and ruin the recipe. Let's face it, we live in a society that places a high value on thinking. From a very early age, we're taught how to think our way out of any situation. We're taught to use our logic and strategize to solve problems and get those things we want. This process starts from the minute you show up for your first day of kindergarten and you need to figure out how to get the teacher's attention. And the rat race begins.

In the school systems in western society, we're trained to think our way through life. The aim and goal is to be smarter than the next guy. There is a lot of cheese down this tunnel when you're playing the 'monopoly of life' game. The guy with the most toys wins, right? The high paying job, the huge house, in the right neighborhood of course, with the 6-car garage. IF that's the game you're playing, being able to out-think the next guy can be a very useful skill.

But there is a trap in over-thinking. You know the old saying, "too much of a good thing"? It's like an artist who is painting a picture. If she keeps looking at the painting and trying to make it better and better, pretty soon it's no good at all. You need to know when enough is enough! Stop thinking and move forward. Easier said than done, I know. We get trapped in our minds – over-thinking constantly. It's like we've got this powerful tool (our brains) and we can't turn it off! And you just want to yell, "Stop the insanity!"

The most common form of this insanity is DDS (doomsday syndrome) – the obsessive worrying about how things could go wrong. A sure sign you know you have DDS is that it's not a matter IF things are going to go wrong, it's a matter of WHEN. The tricky thing about this syndrome is you can easily see it in others, but not so much in yourself. When we see somebody else over-thinking (aka worrying), we think to ourselves, "That's just crazy." But when *we* do it, it makes sense because what *we're* worrying about is justified. I know this all too well. I took my DDS to the next level into OCD (Obsessive Compulsive Disorder), always worrying about what could happen. The 'what if' question and I are great, great friends.

Asking yourself the question, "What could possibly go wrong?" to a point is good. It's a Plan B, and we all know sometimes it's good to have a Plan B to fall back on. But let me be honest.

More often than not, we overdo it. We rewire our brain to

always be on the lookout for pitfalls and anything that is risky.

So our future projecting always ends up being on the negative

side rather than the positive. Wouldn't it be great to think

about all the positive outcomes of a scenario? It definitely

would be better than getting wrapped up in the turmoil of

every possible bad thing that could happen. But it's easy for

most of us to get caught in our own web of worry and "What

if?" And I'm sure this isn't news to you. We as human beings

experience this every day.

Another telltale sign that you might be suffering from DDS is

you keep saying to yourself, "Stop thinking about your

problems!" We actually THINK that might make a difference.

But that's like trying to get rid of a headache by hitting yourself

on the head with a hammer. Thinking to yourself to stop

thinking is just more thinking – are you getting the insanity?

It's like playing that mind game where someone tells you not to think about something like a polar bear in a pink tutu. You find yourself only being able to think of just that!

We can over-think just about anything, big or small. Should I hire that person? Should I follow that marketing plan? Should I write a book? (I over-thought this for seven years.)

You are not to blame for contracting DDS. I not sure if it could have been avoided. We're rewarded for using our brains excessively from a very early age. We are taught to use our brains from Day One. In school, if we struggled for an answer the teacher would bark, "THINK about it. If you THINK about it, the answer will come to you." The only problem is, we weren't taught what to do when the thinking goes amuck. And we weren't taught that analytical thinking and strategizing can only get you so far. It won't really help you discover your purpose or those things that make you truly happy, though it will help you get the job, the house, the car. But there's always going to be that feeling that there's something missing from your life.

You know what I am taking about. You've seen or know someone (maybe even the person sitting in your chair) that has everything society labels as a necessity in order to be happy. But too often they're unfulfilled and unsatisfied. The problem is, we spend way too much energy on strategizing how to get where we want to go and get things we want to have. Then we try to apply that type of thinking to figuring out what we *really* want out of life. But we can't strategize to discover our life's purpose and what we *really* think is important. That all comes from within. It's what gets you most excited and brings you that enthusiasm no matter how illogical it is! If you don't dare to step beyond your boundaries or society's boundaries, you will be bound to that existence – no pun. Once you've figured out your purpose and started down that path, over-thinking will just get in the way.

Over-thinking causes entrepreneurs to get stuck at every stage of their businesses. Often times it is the reason that people don't get started in the first place. A classic example of this is a person in my mastermind group. He was a plumber, but he was certain he didn't want to do that anymore. He wanted to work with people and help them get in touch with their passion through travel and physical activity and experience. But he just couldn't settle on what his next steps should be.

To us, looking at it from outside, it was obvious that he needed to start marketing himself and his idea. How would he start guiding adventures if he didn't have anyone to guide? Obvious, right? But for him, it wasn't obvious at all. He kept getting bogged down in the details of exactly what he was going to do, where he was going to go, financial concerns, what group size would be best – trying to analyze all these decisions that he couldn't possibly make until after he had some potential clients. His perceptual blinders and over-thinking were just keeping him in the dark, creating anxiety out of all the 'what if's'. The action he needed to do first was glaringly obvious to those outside of his sphere of fear. But the anxiety caused by thinking too much was keeping him immobilized. All he really had to do was to get out of the over-thinking phase and simply start taking action.

Too Much Information

We live in an amazing time. We are living in the information age where everything we want to know is right at our fingertips. The internet changed our lives. But even though the internet can be a resourceful tool, it's so easy to get lost in the volumes of information! If you're not careful, you can fall down the rabbit hole, clicking from one site to another until you don't even remember where you began! All these experts with all this information: how to do this, why you should do that, yadda yadda yadda – you know what I'm talking about. There is limitless information on just about anything from a zillion sources. But after a certain point, how useful is it? From my perspective, too much information just muddies the waters and can leave you even more confused with no clear direction for taking action. I speak from experience.

When my partner and I drove from Split to Dubrovnik, Croatia, we were all set; we had a map, there were road signs, and I had printed the directions from the internet. No worries. But about three minutes into the trip, we were lost. There were very few street signs and those were in Greek (well, really Croatian, but it was Greek to us). The road signs and our map didn't seem to agree. Completely frustrated, it was clear that we needed to pick a path. So we chose to follow the road signs. And, as is often the case, when we let go and trusted ourselves, we ended up on the most spectacular road along the Adriatic Sea.

In today's world, we have so many possible directions that keep us stuck: Facebook, email inboxes, Twitter. It can become pretty addictive, can't it?

We're addicted to information; we want to know everything. It becomes a pitfall when we think that *knowing* more is going to *do* more for us—that knowing something is the same as doing something. Watch out for this trap.

It's easy to fall down the rabbit hole because we're barraged with ideas and information, insight and opinion, and constant input that can leave us in a swirl. But as entrepreneurs, at a certain point, we don't need more information or feedback. We need to get back in the flow and take action.

OCD (Overly Creative Disorder) – Too Many Ideas

When people are stuck, especially entrepreneurs, the problem is rarely a lack of ideas. We are a creative lot. The problem is we often have way too many ideas. We suffer from OCD (Overly Creative Disorder), which is way more fun than Obsessive Compulsive Disorder, but still leaves us stuck in the sand. Business owners and entrepreneurs are often bombarded with millions of opportunities or possibilities. Sounds great, right? But if you've ever been there, it can leave you feeling overwhelmed or stuck with all these ideas and all these thoughts running through your head. And the problem is, they are all really great ideas.

A colleague and great friend of mine coaches first time authors in writing their own books. She sees this same problem. "Most people have more than one book in them. But they try to cram it all into one book or they can't figure out which book to start with. I always tell them to pick one idea and run with it. If they don't pick one and stick with it, they end up bouncing around and not getting any of their ideas on paper."

It's because of her you're reading this book. My head was swimming with so many ideas – brilliant ideas, I must say – for what I wanted to write about. I had so much I wanted to share with the world. So many ways that I wanted to make a difference. It was noisy in my head. But Heather had this amazing ability to turn down the noise and have me get clear about what I was committed to. Why did I want to write a book in the first place? Once I answered that question for myself, everything fell into place.

I am not the only one on my team with Overly Creative Disorder; I am surrounded by them. Now, this sounds like a good thing. But if you spend all your time coming up with new ideas and you don't make a decision on which ones to pursue, you end up not getting much of anything done. That's why I hire creative people who love checklists.

A word of warning: people with OCD tend to hang around each other. So if you have OCD, find a "check-lister" to add to the mix. That's what I did.

Rigidity (the curse of being right)

Okay, so what's wrong with being right? We all like to be right, right? How many people do you know who are excited about being wrong? It's human nature. But needing to be right *all* the time can leave us stuck in a couple of ways.

First of all, it makes us afraid to look at information or insight that contradicts our own point of view. We get rigid and put the blinders on – and in the process, we miss a lot of helpful hints and alternatives that could help us get where we want to go more smoothly.

Also, when we hang on to being right all the time, we become afraid to make mistakes. And as every good entrepreneur knows, if you're not making mistakes, you really aren't stretching enough! Fear of making mistakes often shows up in "but that's the way we've always done it." I call it 'habitual thinking', which really means that we take the same rigid worn-out approach to whatever issue comes along.

Another part of being 'right' is that it usually requires that someone else is 'wrong', which is a huge trap! How you relate to others can clearly indicate whether you are stuck in the mindset of needing to be right. Do you find yourself constantly arguing? Defending and proving your point of view? "If I could only get them to understand (or if they were just a little smarter), they would certainly agree with me!"

Maybe you think that you are well adjusted and reasonable. It's just all those *other* people who have a problem. Well, I've got some bad news: they aren't the real problem. Not to say there aren't difficult people out there. But if you are personally

102

reacting in negative ways, whether through action or emotion, you are allowing yourself to be engaged in an unhealthy dynamic – which is not what someone who is unstuck is going to do. There are endless sources of conflict, but your permission – explicit or implicit – is required for you to be involved in any kind of negative discourse at all. Does this mean you shouldn't defend yourself if you are being attacked, be it verbally or physically? Not necessarily. Sometimes you need to make your voice heard or protect your well-being. But if you find that personal attacks of any kind are a part of your everyday life, you need to examine what in your mindset is allowing that unhealthy drama to continue.

In an interpersonal relationship, you are only ever going to be able to control your own actions and reactions. If you are struggling with a partner, client, or subordinate, the first place to look is into your own mindset. Are you being inflexible? Are you projecting outmoded thoughts or unrealistic expectations? Overall, where is your own culpability? Often it comes down to a place of ego or attachment. We may sense that someone is operating from an unhealthy place, or maybe even just a distasteful one, and that can trigger the urge to correct or admonish. We want to 'be right', and we assert that 'rightness' over someone we perceive as 'wrong.' Instead of surrendering to this binary mode of analysis, we should ask ourselves, "What words and actions are best going to help ameliorate the situation? Are we problem-solving or merely being petty and rigid?"

In times of direct disagreement, it can be useful to examine perspective, both your own and the other party's. This serves two functions: discernment of your own motivation and the most direct route to resolution. If you are dealing with an openly hostile person, this can naturally be more difficult. But many times conflicts are due to miscommunication and misinterpretation. Taking ego and fixed modalities of thought off the table can often get the conversation and interaction moving in a positive direction again.

No one ever wants to be the one who is wrong – it's the opposite of right! We live in a world filled with big egos and strong opinions, and if we hear something different than our own opinion, we either speak up or pipe down. But there's always a third option. How about just listening and considering the other person's thoughts? Sometimes we don't know everything, and that's not a bad thing to admit. Even as a solo entrepreneur, one must collaborate with others in order to be successful. It's bull-headedness that keeps you from getting the results you want and leaves you stuck.

Habitual Thinking Exercise

Pick a couple of tasks you want to accomplish and create a plan to make it happen. Your task might be to talk to someone you have wanted to partner with or get advice from, or something you want to learn. Design your

plan and keep a journal as you go through the process you've laid out. We generally have a similar pattern or habit whenever we approach a certain task. We have similar conversation with ourselves and others about it, and we get stuck in very similar ways task after task. After you have journaled the process a few times, see if you can spot a common pattern emerge. The power is in knowing your pattern/habit and those places where you jump tracks.

Next, talk to someone you respect. Ask them how they would approach those same tasks and listen carefully. Notice how their thinking and approach differs from yours. If you are willing to take off your blinders and give up being right, you'll open up a whole new world of possibilities!

Perspective Exercise

You can do this exercise alone, but it's more beneficial to bring in others if you work with a team of people. You'll gain greater insight into your own business by looking at it from their different perspectives. Step back and consider the focus and actions you're currently pursuing in your business. Where have you *not* been getting results? This could be anything from having a buildup of unread and unanswered emails, to the bigger problem of a marketing program that just isn't bringing in business. If it's a particular issue, project or direction that *you* created, be especially careful to not allow your stubborn nature to get the best of you and convince you that (despite all the facts!) you're still in the right. There is always room for improvement, even when you don't think there is.

Gather your team (or people you collaborate with) and *listen* to them. Ask them and yourself, "What's missing?" or if you should be taking different actions. Consider your own strengths as well as your partners and staff. Take a deep breath and allow everything out on the table – no sacred cows! You need to create a safe space for people to be honest with you— particularly if you're the boss. This is the only way you're going to get another perspective, because they've already told you what you want to hear. I promise if you create this space, magic will happen! You'll see the whole picture through fresh eyes. This new perspective is your road map to distinguishing those elements that are not working or are not your strong suit. Being open and flexible allows you to avoid taking further wrong action down an unproductive path. Grinding your tires into the sand gets you back on the road and into motion down a better path.

Avoiding Action

You know those mornings where you wake up and the bed feels so good you just want to stay there all day long? This is pretty much what I think every morning—particularly on those cold winter mornings! I must confess there have been times where I've stayed in bed, not to sleep, but to simply lie there. It feels good for a while, just relaxing and thinking; having no obligations, drifting in and out of sleep. But as the hours drag on, getting up can become challenging. You would think it would be so easy to just get up and get moving. But after hours of avoiding doing just that, we suddenly lose all motivation to do it.

This doesn't just happen with getting out of bed in the morning, it happens in all areas of our lives. We have that same feeling anywhere we lack the motivation to move forward or change our course. Inertia happens, and we just stay stuck. Just like when we stay in bed, we dawdle around for a while, then we trick ourselves into thinking, because we've wasted most of the day, it would be better if we just stayed in bed.

There is always tomorrow, right? If you work for yourself with no time clock or boss waiting for you to show up, this can be especially seductive. "I'll get around to making those calls or changing my website or starting my business" – you get my point. But this is just another mind trap. Taking action, even when you don't want to, is definitely better than being stuck!

In choosing to stay in bed (or play Words with Friends® or reorganize your sock drawer), you're also choosing to pass on possible opportunities. What if that great next client is just one phone call away? Or the solution to that sticky issue is just a few calculations away? What if that perfect collaborative partner is at the networking event you're avoiding?

If you feel like you're plodding along day after day not accomplishing anything, take action. Think of all the possible things you could do to move forward. They don't have to be huge actions, just as long as you are able to complete them on a daily basis. I suggest picking three actions that would impact your business and to do them every day for the next 21 days. Why 21 days? Common wisdom says it takes 21 days to make a habit. Make it a part of your schedule and choose a buddy to keep you accountable.

The great thing about completing your tasks every day for 21 days is that you are going to create momentum. Every day you finish those three actions you'll feel really good about it. You've proven to yourself that you can do it. Once you start taking action in your life, the task that seemed so daunting becomes no big deal. They will simply get done. Change your action, you change your behavior. Change your behavior, it changes your life.

I know this sounds overly simple, but it's true. I saw how powerful this is while I was in Dubrovnik. My partner and I purchased an apartment in Budapest, Hungary, and we've been renovating it from floor to ceiling. We took it down to dirt floors. (I am still not sure how that happened since we're on the top floor, but anyway…) We were just about ready to wrap up the renovation and do the final shooting for a TV show that follows people around while they look to buy properties in a different part of the world (see DesinationAha.com for more on that), and we needed to leave Hungary for a period of time as we didn't have a residence visa. Since we had our dogs Bailey and Brodee with us, we didn't want to fly back to the U.S. (Flying over with them in the airplane cargo section was traumatic enough.) So we decided to go to Croatia and settled on Dubrovnik. I was happy how this was all turning out because it was frickin' (a technical term) cold in Budapest. I am not a big fan of the cold, particularly when I'm schlepping around the city.

So we left Budapest and drove to Croatia right around Christmas. While I loved being in Europe, I was feeling like I was not being very productive. It wasn't like I was staying in bed, but things just weren't moving around me. There were these brilliant plans (even if I say so myself) that I wanted to put into action and nothing was happening with them. They were always getting displaced; something always came up. Not only that, there were personal projects that were on the backburner too, and they had been there for a while; like writing this book.

I decided that since a new year was looming, it was time for me to create a new action plan. Every morning, right after my meditation, I was going to come up with three tasks that would move our company forward and I would make sure that if nothing else got done, those tasks WOULD be accomplished. What's amazing is that not only did those tasks get accomplished, all the other projects that were on the backburner began to move as well. Interesting how that works!

And with that: Stop lying in bed and get active!

Dealing with Obstacles

I have never met an entrepreneur who didn't run into obstacles along the way to fulfilling his or her purpose. Never.

And honestly? Often the bigger the obstacle they face, the more amazing the result they produce in the world. Obstacles (aka challenges) are what builds our mental/emotional/creative muscles. They make us smarter and more capable. They help us hone our products, our systems, our teams. Yet one of the worst mind traps we can fall into is how most of us think about obstacles – as something to be avoided or overcome as quickly as possible! We might take them as signs that we're on the wrong path, that we should stop what we're doing and do something different. But these perspectives will only leave us stuck.

One of my biggest obstacles in business and in life is OCD. Not the Overly Creative Disorder, but the real deal—Obsessive Compulsive Disorder. It first showed up in college. I was driving down the road in my gold Honda Civic hatchback when I hit a bump. I froze. I thought to myself, did I just hit someone? Something normal in my brain that knew it was just a bump didn't kick in and I was suddenly caught in an endless loop. It didn't matter how many times I circled back and saw the hole in the road. It made no difference. I was stuck as stuck can be.

Not only was I stuck with the constant, unstoppable ruminating in my head and its obsessive thoughts, but also with the way the OCD occurred for me like a problem, and I wanted it to simply disappear! I wanted it to go away and stop ruining my life.

I blamed OCD a lot for how my life was going, or should I say, *not* going. This inner struggle went on for many years. But when I really stepped back and took a look, it actually kept me *unstuck* in a lot of different ways. It made me focus more when I talked to people, so I became a terrific listener. I also had so much compassion for what people were going through. I was clear that I had no idea what was happening for them over in their worlds because no one had a clue about what was happening for me in my world. When I stepped back, I began to see my OCD as a gift, an opportunity for me to make a difference, which was impetus for writing this book. Rather than being a problem, the obstacle is my destiny.

People who really play the game of life, who remain unstuck, learn to relish obstacles. As one of my friends who plays golf says, "I used to get bent out of shape when I'd hit my ball into a bunker or would get in a tough lie. But I've come to realize that this is exactly what makes the game so fun. Without the challenges, it would get deadly boring very quickly!"

Obstacles don't have to be as dramatic or as big as OCD. They're anything you THINK is standing in the way of you achieving what you want. We face obstacles every day and our adventures in Hungary illustrate this beautifully.

Two of my biggest passions are real estate and travel. (I shared earlier that my partner and I own a home in Budapest, Hungary.) On one of the trips to Budapest when we were looking for the perfect apartment to buy, I decided to make the most of the trip by interviewing European PR companies for a client who wanted to do an event in Munich. I scheduled

meetings with several different Budapest-based PR companies.

I began with Hill and Knowlton first thing Thursday morning.

So I got myself up early because I had a call with a client in Italy

before the meeting. Being someone who is *never* late, I wanted

to make sure I had plenty of time and wasn't rushed! My client

in Italy couldn't make the call, which gave me even more time. I

was looking good and even ahead of schedule. I love that!

Before leaving, I checked my map and thought I knew exactly

where I was going. I headed to the number 2 tram that runs

along the Danube and has spectacular views of the castle,

Matthew's Church, and passes right by the parliament building.

I was really happy just being out and about in Budapest.

The tram stops right at Margaret Bridge and I was in good

shape for time. So I leisurely strolled through the beautiful

neighborhood. People were walking their dogs, sitting,

enjoying coffees. The weather was magical. I walked in the

general vicinity of where I'm sure that Hill and Knowlton is located. I'm so confident I didn't even bring a map. I figured when I got to the area, I'd just look for the street.

But when I began to nonchalantly look for the street, I couldn't find it. So I thought, "Maybe I just need to walk a little further." Still no familiar street names. My leisurely stroll started to become a quick stride. I thought, "Maybe I should just cancel the meeting." I was further out from the city by then and not sure what to do. You know those moments when you have to choose whether to stay on the track you've chosen or bail? I decided to stay on the track. I saw a real estate office and thought, "Perfect! They are going to know the area and speak English."

I walked in and said, "Excuse me." The receptionist got a distressed look on her face. Uh oh. She said something to her colleague who turned and spoke to me in English. Whew! I pulled out my pad where I had scribbled my directions and asked her if she knew that street. She looked confused. A man walked by and they all began to speak in Hungarian. He looked confused. He pulled out his computer and consulted the holy grail, Google, while she pulled out a map. Finally, they determined that I was on the wrong side of the Danube. Sh&%#t! They handed me a map and drew big circles around my destination as if somehow the big circles would keep this ignorant American from getting lost again.

Walking out of the real estate office, I had another of those moments of choice. I had 20 minutes to walk back about a mile so I could catch the tram across the bridge, take another commuter rail, and the walk another mile to the office. I decided to go for it! So I sprinted through the streets of Pest, weaving through the locals who clearly did not share my same sense of urgency.

Sweaty and winded, I arrived and boarded the tram to take me across the bridge. The clock said 10:48 am and my meeting was at 11:00 am. This might be doable! I might be just fashionably late. Across the bridge, I dashed to the commuter train only to hit the platform just as the train is pulling out of the station. %^&$! Really! So I stood fuming and waiting for the post-communist train to arrive. I was clear at this point I was going to be late, but the question now was how late? Fashionably or rudely?

We reached my stop and I started to walk in the direction of the office. The feature that makes the Buda side so beautiful is that it is hilly, which also makes it inconvenient for walking. As I trekked up the hills, I was becoming discouraged. "I am going to be so late. So what's the point of even trying?" I was thinking about turning around, explaining what happened, and rescheduling. But just then, I looked up. Right in front of me is a restaurant called Wasabi. Is that a sign or what? I mean come on! Right in the middle of Budapest is a restaurant named after our PR company? Well, okay, maybe it was named after the Japanese mustard – but I'm just sayin'...

So I decided to keep going at least until the next major street. As soon as I made that decision, I spied a tiny side street. It was the street I'd been trying to find for what seemed like decades!

So I finally walked into the office and looked at the clock: I was only 15- 20 minutes late. The person I was to meet greeted me with, "No problem. You are just on Budapest time." The meeting was amazing and her insights on PR and marketing were incredible – and exactly what I needed to hear.

So what's the lesson? For me, I saw that in that moment that, when we are present, we get to see what is running the show. And we get to see what/who is doing the choosing. We get to experience where we have the opportunity to stay in the flow despite the obstacles or challenges. On my journey, I could clearly see those moments when I could have chosen to give up. The thing that could have stopped me was my not wanting to look bad. But by staying present, I could choose what was most important to me. As entrepreneurs, we always have to ask ourselves, "Who and what is running the show?"

Here's a sports analogy to make my point. (I know, I'm quite impressed that I can come up with a sports analogy.)

Wasabi Publicity is made up of a bunch of adrenaline junkies!

How cool is that? Shannon, our CFO, may be the craziest. He

has several hobbies that a 'normal' person would deem as

insane. Kayaking tops the list He paddles class V rivers – and

for those of you who don't know what that means, basically it's

the equivalent of throwing yourself off a waterfall. When he's

kayaking, the river is full of obstacles where he could get stuck.

Some rapids are full of rocks and hydraulics (which is a

technical term and I don't know what it means either) that can

beat up even the best of navigators. The way he looks at the

river and the way that a new kayaker would look at the river

are completely different – because for Shannon, the obstacles

for the new kayaker are opportunities for him. An obstacle is

not to be feared, but embraced. In fact, he sees obstacles as an

opportunity to take his kayaking to the next level. When we

feel trapped and things seem impossible, there is no freedom

and all our focus is on the obstacles. We try to avoid them. But

what we resist, persists. If you plan to get back into the flow of

the river, you have to adopt a new mindset and approach all

your obstacles like Shannon does, as an integral and exciting part of the whole adventure!

In the Realm of Overwhelm

We have all had those moments, when the world seems to be closing in. You have the weight of the world on your shoulders and you don't know which way to turn. You are completely paralyzed. Coffee or tea seems like a monumental decision. I'm not talking about those frustrating days we all have from time to time, where nothing seems to be going according to plan and you just want to go home and get back in bed. I'm talking about when you hit the wall and you don't know how to move forward.

Your mind is racing a mile a minute, your breathing is shallow, and there's too much going on. You've reached a point of complete overwhelm and you're living in a swirl. Everything begins to look like a problem. Your mindset switches frequency and tries to escape by any means possible. At the front of the list is procrastination. It kicks in and we let it comfortably take over. We find any excuse to escape taking action even if it's as unrelated as "Did I leave my stove on again?" I sure hope not!

This is a slippery slope and once things start getting a little rocky, our minds have us racing around and we end up getting ourselves lost. It's here that our reality becomes warped by over-generalizing and blowing things out of proportion. I'd be a millionaire by now if I had a quarter for every time I've heard someone say, "I have *sooo* much work." Sometimes it's true, but mostly we feel that way when we find ourselves stuck. It's when we start exaggerating our reality that we end up convincing ourselves that it's true. Each time we say it, a signal is sent to our subconscious to take note of this stressor. We get so wrapped up that we ultimately find ourselves paralyzed. When overwhelm gets the better of us, we start to create false realties of what we think is so, rather than what is *actually* so.

Think of it this way: your feeling of overwhelm is like the story of "The Wizard of Oz." You, Dorothy, have been caught in a tornado and find yourself in the dreamlike Land of Oz. You're living in a temporarily created false reality until you are ready to wake up and return back to Kansas. And just like the characters of the Scarecrow, Tin Man, and the Cowardly Lion, you're on a journey to find a way back to 'reality'. So you follow the yellow brick road to find out what you think is missing or incomplete. While it might be fine to stop and take a quick nap in the poppies, if you want to get back home, you can't keep making excuses for why you shouldn't take action.

The most common cop-outs I hear are either "I'm too busy" or "I don't have enough money." With this mentality, you start to miss out on potential opportunities that may be coming down the pike. Again, maybe these excuses are legitimate. But a majority of the time, we say these things because we haven't looked at the bigger picture.

BEING PRESENT

Bottom line: If you are living anywhere other than in the present, you are stuck. Period. Pretty strong statement, huh? I've seen the difference in my own life and career when I focus on staying fully in the present – and the difference is amazing.

We constantly hear about 'being fully in the present' from personal growth gurus and spiritual leaders. There are all kinds of practices to help us get there. But what is this 'being present' thing anyway? How could we 'live' anywhere but in the present? So why does it seem to be a place we need to get back to?

For me, living in the present has a few components. First of all, it is when our focus is fully here and now. In other words, we aren't regretting the past or worrying about the future. Second, it's when we are relaxed and calm enough to be completely aware of what's going on in the present moment. We're aware of the environment, our reactions, our thoughts, as well as the energy of people around us. And within that awareness is a sense of being objective and non-judgmental, which allows us to perceive choices in how we respond to what is happening in the present moment. Also, to me, living in the present means that all your faculties are present and accounted for. You are present in this very moment physically, mentally, and emotionally.

Being fully present is not just a place that you hit when you're sitting cross-legged on a cushion in a deep state of meditation. Athletes and creative types call it The Zone, and they value it as the state that makes them the most productive and successful. In some ways, I think it's a very natural state that somehow we've gotten away from.

As I'm writing this, I'm watching the 2012 Summer Olympics. Isn't it fascinating to witness the world's premier athletes in action? What's the difference between these highly skilled athletes and a rank amateur? Both have the understanding of the game, but it's the training and especially the mindset that makes one stand out over the other. For example, if you're a mid-level tennis player, you know how it feels to see a speeding ball coming right at you. It's pretty scary and there's almost no time to react.

But a professional athlete experiences the game in a totally different way. They don't fear the ball. Rather they watch it with intent, all their faculties engaged as they calculate the proper return shot. Everything slows down. Some report that the lines of the ball even align with their racket. It's the same ball, but a very different perspective than the perspective of an amateur player. The pro moves naturally, knowing exactly what to do next with no hesitation. And in your life, once you start looking at the things from the 'what's so' perspective, you will be clear on what actions you'll need to take to get yourself back on track.

Even though you would think that simply living in the present should be no big deal, it is. Most of us are living in the past or the future, or we're living in our heads while our emotions are set adrift. Or we're seeing everything through our emotional reactions so we aren't really aware of what's truly happening around us. For the most part, many of us ignore our bodies until it's time to eat or exercise. We get into treating our bodies like some vehicle whose only purpose is to carry our brains around! We rush around so much that we feel like we don't have time to be 'mindful' in everything we do. Don't you have to be a Buddhist monk and live in a monastery or something like that to be mindful and fully present in every moment?

No. I've found it does take some focus and motivation to practice staying in the present. But the costs of *not* being present are huge. Understanding these costs might be all the motivation you need!

Being Aware

You may think that you are seeing your whole reality before you, but your brain is subconsciously choosing for you what you want to see. If you ever took Psych 101 back in college, you might remember learning about the Gestalt theory – how our brains group information in order to best and most efficiently make sense of it. If we *didn't* do that, we couldn't get through the day. As an example, we've all noticed what happens when someone starts talking about the blinking of our eyes. Suddenly we notice those little microsecond blackouts when we blink. Most of the time, it goes on without us noticing those blacked out periods at all. Can you imagine how annoying it would be to be constantly conscious of those blacked out moments?

Because there's so much data bombarding us at any point in time, our brain actually figures out what data to completely ignore and what to focus on. In other words, the phrase 'creating your reality' isn't just some New Age mantra. It's a factual statement regarding human perception. We are always 'creating our reality' through the data that we choose to perceive, accept, and prioritize in our consciousness. So the reality you choose to live is just made up of a series of your chosen perceptions; and what you don't notice gets left behind in the dust.

You may be thinking right now, "But I know what's real. I'm objective about where the truth lies." Yes, likely you have a basic grasp on reality. I'm not trying to insinuate that you are hallucinating. But the reality you perceive on a day-to-day basis is just that – a reality that is perceived. It is a reality made up of your perceptions and the subsequent processing of those perceptions. It's the old 'glass half-full' idea – but I'm not just talking about attitude. I'm talking about whether or not you are actually seeing and noticing what you need to see and notice – whether you even see the glass is *there*, never mind what's in it. Basically, it's about how *consciously aware* you are.

One analogy I find helpful is getting dressed in the morning.

Imagine waking up in the morning, rolling out of bed, doing your normal morning routine. At some point, you pull on a pair of pants. As you first start to pull on your pants, you notice the material against your body. It might feel soft or cool, or even a little scratchy. But unless you are totally engrossed in something else, odds are that you will notice the pants and the fact that they are on. This awareness will probably occur for about 3 or 4 seconds, tops.

Then you're going to mentally move on, right? Because unless the pants are on fire, once you identify the material and acknowledge that you are now wearing clothes, your mind is basically going to decide to forget about your pants for the day. You don't need to keep acknowledging the fact that you're wearing them, so you don't. They are on your body –mission accomplished! It's time for your brain to move on to more important things.

Now, generally speaking, this is a good thing, brain-wise. Your mind takes in data, "does its thing" with that data, and then puts it to the top of your priority list, or it doesn't, and it stays there at the top of that list, or it doesn't. If we went around thinking about our pants all day, we wouldn't get very much done, now would we? If you continued to acknowledge "Yep. My pants are on!" and continued to notice how the material felt against your legs, that would be extremely distracting.

Given that your brain's processing power is finite, you can only process so much data at a given time. Mere sensual data would overload you constantly if you didn't filter it out somehow. So it makes sense to clear your conscious mind of your pants once they're on and zipped up. But the point is that *everything is like the pants.* A strange concept, I know, but that's exactly how it works: Your mind takes in data, deals with it, prioritizes it, and then often pushes it out of your conscious awareness to make room for something more critical.

But what happens when we stop seeing the things that are making us feel uncomfortable? Things that might be warning signs or directional signals for us? Back to the pants: What if those pants aren't the right pants? What if they are little too short, or a little too long, or a little too tight, or a little too loose, and you really shouldn't be wearing them at all? What if they *used* to be your favorite pants, but you have outgrown them in some way?

For many of us, the only time you are going to even notice and act on that feeling is *right when you put them on.* If you didn't prioritize right then that they were making you uncomfortable, and change out of them right when they had your attention, there is a good possibility that you are just going to stop consciously noticing the discomfort over the course the day. You'll just live with them and that feeling. You may not realize that they are why you feel a little cranky or uncomfortable, and could even blame your mood on something totally different, when it really is just that the pants aren't working out for you anymore.

What gets us stuck is that we choose to keep the pants on instead of changing them when we first notice the problem. It doesn't seem like a big deal and we think we're too busy to do anything about them. Like a lot of other things in our lives, we decide to ignore or adapt to the slight discomfort. Our brains take that input and help us to stop consciously noticing unease over the course the day. So we learn to live with those uncomfortable pants. Sure, there are times when this approach can be a good thing. But if we do it too much with too many uncomfortable feelings, eventually we start feeling numb and zoned out to our realities. We become unaware of our own feelings and our environment.

Initially, it seems easier to let those little niggling issues be. But if you're stuck, you need to look at all data you are taking in consciously and unconsciously and what you are doing with it. You need to become aware – calmly and objectively – of all that is in your internal and external environment. That awareness will give you the information you need to take appropriate action to get yourself unstuck.

I had a classic experience of the power of this on a conference call recently. After I shared my excitement about being here in Budapest, the next person said, "I was just wondering when Drew is going to shut up and stop bragging." Ouch! I was a little taken back. Okay, a little more than taken back– I was stunned. I had been sharing about my life here in Budapest and this huge opportunity to tap into the amazingly talented Hungarian people. I thought I was sharing my excitement, but at least one person felt that I was bragging.

My first reaction was to pull away from the group. But by staying calm and paying attention, I noticed that pulling away was a very common theme when I face this type of situation. I feel fine if I'm misunderstood and have the chance to refine what I say and leave them with what I meant to express. But when it feels like a personal attack, that is a whole other story. I thought back to other experiences where my choice has been to retreat, and I realized that I might have missed out on some good opportunities. That's when I realized that the comment might not have anything to do with me. I know we like to think everything is about us. But the truth is that it's not. As much as we like to think that we have control over how another person reacts, we don't. And much as we would like to blame other people for how we react, they are not to blame. With this newfound awareness, I was able to create a different way to respond rather than pulling away. And the interesting thing is that later the same person shared with me that he was jealous, and that's why he said what he said. It didn't have anything to do with me.

Pants Exercise

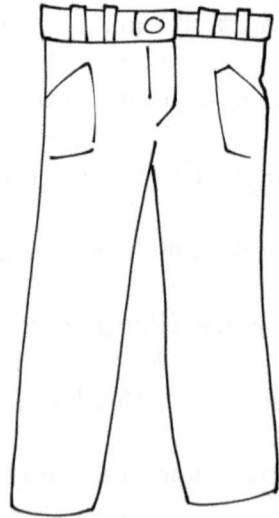

With all this talk about pants, this exercise calls for you to find that one item of clothing that you've avoided throwing out. That's right, I'm calling you out! I think we're all vain enough to keep holding on to that one great pair of pants that doesn't fit anymore. I know I have a pair. So go into your closet and slip (yank?) those babies on. Now either you're looking at yourself in the mirror thinking you never looked better or you're feeling uncomfortable and awkward, right?

Well, if you're feeling uncomfortable, keep that feeling in mind and think about your business. Is there some place in your business where this vague feeling of 'not right' comes up? You might not have even realized that you've been feeling uncomfortable. You may have just tuned out those feelings or thought it better to suck it up than to address the issue. You're ignoring the problem to the point where you've become numb to it but it's still bothering you and undermining your energy and your efforts.

If nothing pops up as immediately as a pair of too-tight pants, keep musing about it. You can start by thinking of the things we've already discussed – your purpose, values, and what's important to you. Are you and those things being fulfilled? If

139

not, is it because you've gotten use to feeling unsatisfied? Your business 'pants' problems can come from a number of things. It could be the people you've been working with or the fact you've been doing things that you're not good at doing. It could simply be that you've gotten in the habit of procrastinating or working reactively rather than proactively. Focus your awareness on areas of vague discomfort in your business. Don't let yourself get distracted. Be brave and know that it just might be time to throw those pants out and buy a new pair! Or maybe you need to take a different action like hitting the gym so you can fit into them again without that ugly muffin top! Either way, make a plan to address that discomfort *now*, not later. Until you take action, you're going to keep feeling that tight elastic band around your waist.

In the future, as you increase living fully in the present moment, your heightened awareness will help you catch that vague discomfort earlier. Make it a habit to address the issues as soon as you start feeling uncomfortable – and watch how much more energy and enthusiasm you have!

What's Your Time Zone?

Have you ever watched your pet dog or cat throughout the day? They definitely live in the present moment. Your cat sees a sunny spot so she wanders over to it and takes a nap. She doesn't worry about how long that sunny spot will last or if it's as warm as the sun spot three days ago. You pull out the leash and your dog leaps in wild joy. He doesn't sulk because you neglected to take him walking yesterday or hesitate because he's not sure if he'll like the route. Our pets simply stay in the present.

But we human animals tend to live in either the past or the present. Our bodies are located in the present moment (where else could they go?!?) but our thoughts and emotions are too often focused elsewhere. Where are you located right now? Physically, you might be at the office or maybe at home. But when you're feeling stuck, you are mentally and emotionally absent to all things present. It's like crossing a busy street before the signal tells you to go: if you're not paying attention, you're likely to get hurt. And when we focus in the past or the future, more often than not we're creating fear, doubt, and anxiety for ourselves, right?

I had an experience, what we might call "a bad day," recently that showed me the value of staying in the present. One morning I came into the office early to shoot a video. First, the video camera didn't work. Then we got it working, but the delivery guy showed up to deliver my new computer right in the middle of the shoot. Then my computer sound didn't work. The list went on and on and on. A twenty-minute project took up most of the day. You've had those days, right?

If I had been stuck in the past or future, my internal dialogue would have gone something like this: "This always happens to me! Just like last time, nobody bothered to check the equipment. Why can't the delivery guy ever come when he says he will? (I'm not sure when that is, but it's not when I'm shooting a video.) Now that everything is off-kilter, it will probably be a disaster, just like that video we made last year. And now how will I ever get the rest of my work done? And . . . and . . . and . . ." Sound familiar?

But the good news was that I wasn't stuck this time. I stayed in the present moment and experienced the freedom and flow there. I felt a little "Grrr," but it was mild and didn't have a lot of internal chatter with it. I was able to make rational decisions about what to do in the situation and everything came out fine with no stress or hassle. Had I been stuck in past or future, it would have been a completely different scenario.

Stuck in the Past

As Tony Robbins said, "Everybody's got a past. The past does not equal the future unless you live there." But many of us mistakenly use the past as a measure of what is possible in the present and future. Just because your meeting, call, plan, or (you fill in the blank) didn't go the way you want, you think the next *blank* is going to go the same way. We begin to tell ourselves a story, a story that always has the same ending. It's not the telling of the story that's the problem... the problem is that we begin to believe it.

One of the many things I admire about Michelle is she always catches herself when she's telling herself a past-based story. Maybe it's because she tells our clients' stories to the media day after day that she sees the plot of her own story so quickly. And if she needs help rewriting the story, she picks up the phone. Michelle calls me every once in a while when she has a call with the media that doesn't go according to plan. The media person, for whatever reason, is short or rude – probably nothing personal to Michelle – but when you're on the other end, it sometimes feels personal.

Most the time she just shakes it off. But if she finds herself beginning to dance to a story that doesn't empower her and it begins to occur like the truth, she picks up the phone. We talk until she's clear what happened is just what happened and it doesn't have any bearing on how her next call will go.

When it comes to thinking of the past, for the most part, we usually end up thinking of our highest and lowest points. You'd think that your lowest points would be the only source to all your troubles, but even your past accomplishments can wrack up a lot of anxiety. In either case, we become too preoccupied with what *has* happened. Obviously, we'd never want to return to any of our bad experiences. Yet we can get stuck replaying them either to ourselves or (even worse) out loud to others. Rather than learning the lesson and moving on, we re-run it and re-experience it in all its painful detail. It's like we're rehearsing ourselves for the next time! We assume (wrongly) that if we were unsuccessful in the past, we are likely to be unsuccessful in the future.

Even fixating on a past success can make you obsess on how to get it back. "How come I'm not as successful/fit/wealthy/creative as I was before?" We want to argue with the nature of reality. Everything is always changing; nothing stays the same. You were a different person hopefully fulfilling the things that were important to you then, but that doesn't mean those same things are still important to you. If you find they truly are the same, searching for clues as to what is different in the present can be helpful. But typically, we're just using our successful past to beat ourselves up in the present and this just causes a downward spiral. It's like having a nervous tick that constantly has you thinking about it over and over again. Rather than actually taking action and moving forward in the present, our mindset keeps us drifting backwards into the past.

Don't let past rejection or failure dictate what is going to happen to you in the present or even the future. The value of the past is to learn its lessons and grow from them. Unless you truly are looking to the past to help yourself, you are indulging in a terrible cycle by constantly replaying it. If something in your past needs to be healed or fixed or reconciled, the only place you can do it is in the present, right? So if there is some action you need to take about the past, take it and be done with it. If not, put the past where it belongs.

Stuck in the Future

There are a couple of ways we can get stuck in the future. One is what I call "the someday, one day syndrome." It's when you hold off doing something or being something until you have enough money or get that degree or have enough time or the economy is right or – get the drift? We're wasting our time sitting on the dock, waiting for our boat to come in. Most entrepreneurs understand that you've got to jump in and swim toward that boat!

I heard a story once of a guy who kept praying to God, "Please let me win the lottery." Day after day he would pray, until finally, one day, God answered back, "Buy a lottery ticket."

In the PR game, I see a lot of people who don't buy lottery tickets. I listen intently as they outline for me all their elaborate plans of how they're going to write a book, have their own TV show, and ultimately change the world. It's clear they've spent hours and hours fantasizing about their dream life. I'm hooked, so I ask them, "What's in play to achieve that?" Usually there's a long awkward pause until they reply, "Well, as soon as I have the (fill in the blank), I'll get started."

Stop waiting around for opportunities. You must go out and create them yourself. Don't scam yourself into thinking that success, like a shining prince on a white horse, will come your way if you wait long enough. Odds are that prince is busy with the people who got on their horses and chased him down! Once you change your mindset, the actions you take in the present will naturally flow into the workings of your future. This way, you are creating your own future rather than crossing your fingers and hoping for the best.

Another way we can get stuck in the future is the "what if" trap. Because I have OCD, this cycle is painfully familiar to me. I've seen firsthand how it knocks me out of the present. For sure when I'm dealing with my obsessive thoughts, I know that I'm

not living in the present moment. I'm busy worrying about

some future catastrophic event that may or may not happen,

playing out all the worst-case scenarios. And honestly, it isn't

any fun!

Too many entrepreneurs let these persistent thoughts get

them stuck. Worrying about the future just surrounds them in

fear and doubt in the present. So they don't make the phone

calls they need to make or they don't take the risks they know

they should take because they're focusing on that worst-case

scenario, just like the plumber in my mastermind group. He

projected into the future that he might fail so he became frozen

by inaction. If you spend your time fearing the worst, it's like

you've got your foot on the brakes and are driving 45 miles an

hour down the freeway – while all the good opportunities pass

you in the fast lane.

There is of course a very positive way to use future thinking.

Most successful people look at the future and have a very

powerful interpretation or vision of how they want it to turn out. But they're really in the flow of it, feeling empowered by where they're heading, yet living life fully in the present moment. Unstuck.

About Fear

"The only thing we have to fear is fear itself." ~ Franklin D. Roosevelt

If you're stuck, the reason you are stuck is fear. I know this is a very bold statement. But if you stop and think about it, fear is the quicksand of our life. If you're stuck, there is no action. And what other reason could there be for you not taking action other than fear? You may be saying to yourself, what if I'm confused? Being confused doesn't mean you're stuck, it means that you're confused. You are only stuck when you are not taking action to clarity. And the only reason you are not seeking clarity is fear. This might be good news or bad. It makes finding a solution very easy. It also, however, means that you're going to have to get honest with yourself and confront your fear.

Why are we so afraid? It comes down to biology and our internal survival mechanisms. Our amygdala (that primal part of our brain) is constantly on the lookout for danger and ways to protect us. And when something happens that we perceive as bad, it gets stored in our subconscious and we wait for the alarm to go off again. We look into the future to anticipate potential danger and figure out strategies to avoid it. Even when we've already figured how to avoid getting our VW stuck in the sand, we end up triggering that subconscious stress signal anyways without even committing the crime.

We all are taught from an early age that we are supposed to learn from our mistakes, but learning doesn't discount the fear of it happening again. It is why we get stuck over and over again. Even though, rationally, you *know* that failure won't kill you and you have the potential to create great things, that very visceral fear and anxiety feeling stops you from doing what you know you need to do.

Instead of spinning your tires in the sand, bluff yourself through it. It seems scary, but one of the biggest life lessons I've learned is to just "do the fear."

We all can become complacent and try to avoid the unknown and somewhat scary situations. But that stance will leave you in the dust behind those 'adventurers' who are willing to reframe those fears and leap through them. As Erma Bombeck said, "Worry is like a rocking chair. It gives you something to do, but it gets you nowhere."

Every entrepreneur I've ever known loves the excitement, the passion, and the adrenalin rush of building and growing a business. But the other side of the coin is often fear and anxiety. It is rare that I have seen an entrepreneur who has gained total mastery over the fear and anxiety. But the successful ones know that the most juice lies just behind that fear, so they don't let it stop them. If you're stuck, ask yourself, "What am I afraid of?" Don't be afraid to go to those places that scare you. It is those places where you're going to find happiness. Continue to see those things that scare you, set them up as adventures, and just do them.

For example, having decided to set up shop in Hungary, I am now in a strange land. I'm still not totally sure how they do business here, but I've chosen to see it as really exciting rather than intimidating. I feel like I'm on a great adventure with all the fun, creativity, excitement, and energy that brings. As I make appointments to meet with companies here, it takes me right back to when Michelle and I started Wasabi Publicity and I had to get on the phone and make cold calls. Back then, I was worried about making the calls. But when I picked up the phone, I noticed there was a lot of energy and excitement. Just like kayaking down a river, you get your adrenaline pumping and just go with the flow of the experience. I could walk into my next meeting and I may or may not be able to communicate well. A lot of things might get lost in translation – or it might go great! But my objective is to let go, get into the flow, and let it take its course as I enjoy the ride.

Warming Up the Cold Call

A task right at the top of the anxiety list for most entrepreneurs is cold calling. Just the thought of picking up that phone and your breath quickens and your palms begin to sweat. And that's just the thought of it. I think it's safe to say you may not see cold calling as an exciting adventure, but it's possible to switch your mindset and make it an enjoyable experience. Of course, there are a number of reasons why people don't like to do cold calling: you might be interrupting them, they might reject you, or they might be rude. All these things are possible. But what is the problem? It's not a problem that they happen; the problem is you make it personal. Their reaction doesn't have anything to do with you.

We are in the dialing and smiling business. That is what publicists do – even in this digital age where people communicate in 140 characters or less. What produces the results at the end of the day for our clients is our team getting on the phones – in the trenches, building relationships with the media. If we stopped every time a member of the media is having a bad day or was rude to us on the phone, we would not be successful and our clients would not make the difference they're committed to making.

The way Michelle keeps her head in the game is to create games. Her latest game is she puts a sticker on a map of the U.S. every time she makes a contact in the top 20 markets. It helps her stay present to the bigger picture and ensures she doesn't take it so personally when a journalist is having a bad day and takes it out on her. None of your reasons why you don't like cold calling really matters if you have the right mindset. It starts with staying in the present moment, not projecting into a disappointing future that may or may not happen.

That sounds pretty simple, but people worry so much about the outcome of the call that they don't really take action in the moment.

What totally shifted my attitude towards making cold calls was reframing them in my mind. I realized that cold calling wasn't about convincing the person on the other end of the line to work with us. It was really about having a conversation to see if we *should* be working together by getting to know each other, and sorting through what we each needed and wanted. It was a collaboration, not just me trying to sell them. By changing my mindset, the context of the call was completely transformed. It was not about getting a client – it was about seeing if it was a fit. As much as you want to gain clients, seeing if they are a fit is really important. I never worry about enrolling clients. It is either a fit or it's not a fit; we either should be working together or we should not. It really is that simple.

There is a lot of talk about an evolution happening in business these days. We are moving into a relationship-based economy. I'm seeing the shift. It is not about going out to find and land clients. It's about building relationships and fulfilling your purpose. Wasabi Publicity has always been guided by our intention to support people who want to make a difference in the world. We always trust that we will end up working with the people we should be. We don't have to worry about who we are going to be working with, so my cold calls are really about making connections and building relationships that will make a difference.

Fear as Motivation?

Which is more effective, the carrot or the stick? Though the 'stick' of fear is prevalent in many cultures, including our own, I feel like it's time to outgrow it. Growing up, many of us were more motivated by the fear of punishment or failure than by the rewards of success and accomplishment. We've taken that fear-based motivation into our professional lives. But that kind of motivation can only get us so far and it comes with the price

of stress and constant dissatisfaction. Many entrepreneurs

constantly look over their shoulders, always having to create

and get bigger and better. But that also means they never stop

and feel satisfied about their accomplishments, no matter how

successful they have become.

Fear-based motivation tends to make us less creative and more

risk averse. We're so busy avoiding mistakes that we miss

great opportunities and don't perform our best. If you're a

golfer, think about the difference in hitting a shot in fear of

going in the water versus hitting that same shot motivated by

getting it as close to the pin as you can. Mentally, emotionally,

and physically, those are two totally different experiences.

Think about making a pitch to a potential client with the goal of

not failing versus the goal of having a meaningful and fun

interaction that makes the other party thrilled to work with

you. Notice the difference? Your ability to be effective increases

tremendously when you are motivated by the carrot rather

than the stick. If nothing else, being constantly motivated to move forward by your fears simply doesn't feel good!

Beyond Fear: Seeing Opportunities and Possibilities

Once you start doing what you fear and stop using the past or future to determine if you'll be successful or not, you have given yourself a broader view of the full picture. For me, meditation gives me a broader view by tapping into my higher consciousness. It doesn't matter how limited my thinking has become. When I take my seat and begin to meditate, my perspective shifts immediately. Your conscious mind is only able to process a limited amount of data, so the subconscious mind filters it all and allows you to consciously perceive only certain bits of information and ignore the rest. This keeps you sane on a day-to-day level. But connecting with your higher conscious mind opens up your perception again so you can be present to the whole world of possibilities.

One of the pitfalls for entrepreneurs is tunnel vision. Eager and goal oriented, we get overly fixated on a certain result or expectation. That fixation usually leads to being caught up in all the details rather than taking purposeful, meaningful action. But when you tap into higher consciousness with your intention and purpose in the forefront, your broad perspective allows you to see all kinds of opportunities and assistance that you would have missed before.

When you're unstuck, you're living in a world where everything is possible. Everything around you really occurs as a possibility, not a mistake or a problem. When you're in a state of possibility and everything is possible, you don't stress or struggle when inevitable breakdowns happen and problems occur. You actually see them as possibility, like that professional tennis player who sees the ball coming at them as the next big opportunity rather than a problem that needs to be handled "or else." Life actually slows down in that perspective. When you're stuck, you don't see opportunities when they show up on your doorstep. When you're unstuck, you do.

STRUCTURE & RESOURCES

Now it's time to talk about the 'material world.' Not Madonna's world, YOUR business material world. Just so we're clear, science has proven there really isn't a material world. But we're going to discuss it like it exists, because you most likely believe that it does (like we all do most of the time).

In this section, we'll talk about some of the approaches to your business and material world things that could be making you stuck. Honestly, if you're really clear about your mental/emotional/perceptual stuckness (the internal), the rest of it (the external) just falls into place. But it's worth talking about the issues and fixes most common to entrepreneurs. My suggestion is that you focus first and foremost on the internal, then check out what might be causing your stuckness in the external.

Structure

Because it is so fundamental to the way in which we function, we use the word 'structure' to mean a lot of different things. It can be a verb, as in how you structure your day or your business, or a noun, meaning the vast web of physical or mental building blocks and inter-relationships. It could even be a physical space that is limiting you. But more often, it will be the underlying structure of your business, or the methodology you are using to bring your product or message out to the market. Examining the way you are set up structurally is key to maximizing and expanding your business – to getting to the next level.

One of the most important things to remember about structure is that the ones we create for ourselves and our businesses are not meant to be rigid and unyielding. Scientists have discovered that even concrete structures, like buildings and desks and lampposts, are made up of rapidly moving energy

particles. Everything is in flux, and nothing is actually solid. So

rigidity in anything is counter to the natural state of things.

When we say everything is "flowing along" or we're "going

with the flow," it's a subtle acknowledgement that motion and

flexibility is the best state to operate from. But when we feel

trapped, we use rigid language. "Our back is up against the

wall" or we are "caught between a rock and a hard place."

It's amazing to me how often people (and their businesses) are

imprisoned in self-created cages because they refuse to bend

the bars even the slightest bit. Especially as an entrepreneur,

you should be in charge of your structure, not the other way

around. What are the signs that you are being controlled by

structure? Are you saying things like "We've always done it this

way"? "Things are fine (code for "putting up with &^%$!") the

way they are"? That isn't going to work out. Because if you

aren't moving forward, pretty soon you'll be heading

backwards, particularly within the context of marketing. And whatever structures you are functioning within now have to expand and morph to keep up with the business you are creating.

Here's an example. It's been years since I got an email from a client that was upsetting. The kind that accuses my team for not following through on what was requested. The kind that tells me the ship is sinking and it's our fault entirely. I received one recently.

In my client's world, we were the only plausible explanation for the Titanic's fate. From our vantage point on the lido deck, things occurred quite differently.

The story goes like this. When the ship began to sail, we set the course and we all agreed on the direction we were headed. Our recommendation was to avoid excursions in the itinerary. We set off, busting our butts to get where we needed to be. Along the way, the client decided he wanted to add excursions. So, of course, we served him. The waters were a little rough along the way. The client failed to follow through on requests made by our team, communication was challenging... but I'm sure these things were unintentional oversights.

So there I was, caught between a proverbial rock and the hard place. Blaming the lack of results on the requested excursion, and the lack of communication, would look very much like justification. What do you do? Just as I did, you have a choice. You can get wrapped up in the defense swirl or you can step back to see if there's a lesson to be learned.

Truthfully, I did a little of both.

I felt myself wanting to get sucked up in the swirl. The force was strong. But, I decided instead I would continue to be of service to the client and provide whatever was possible. As for myself, I started to look long and hard at how I was running my own company. For example, taking my team on excursions and not really following the course. And by doing this, I started to feel accountable as the 'captain' that we didn't arrive at our destination.

Whether you're managing a team or working for yourself – it happens: suddenly you're following the yellow brick road when you weren't even planning a trip to Oz. Instead of blaming everything or everyone for you being in Oz, stop first and ask yourself who's feet carried you along that path.

Resources

The word 'resources' can refer to a lot of different things. It can refer to financial resources, human resources, even the resources that you yourself have within you – your talents, skills, character, and experience. Resources and structure are interwoven in life and your business, so I'll be interweaving them in this section as well.

Entrepreneurs tend to be DIYers (do it yourselfers), so the issue of bringing in resources for support can be a thorny one. But if you're operating in the world like you have to do it all yourself, that is a sure telltale sign that you're stuck. Another issue is that, as small businesses, we sometimes get into the mindset of working on a shoestring budget. We typically don't have huge budgets and we tend to be conservative (okay, stingy really) about spending what we have until it is absolutely, undeniably necessary. It for sure has been a balancing act with Wasabi.

My partner Michelle and I started the business a little over ten years ago based on our commitment to work with people who are committed to making a difference in the world. When we opened our doors, it was just Michelle and me. That's it. The two of us were Wasabi Publicity. We created a plan, which included a lot of cold calling. Yay! (Not my initial reaction.) But I quickly reframed it and it was like... swoosh! We landed our first contract almost immediately and we were off to the races. Our business was booming, it all felt congruent, and we were operating in a nice flow. It was literally like a greased slide.

But in order for us to keep growing and make an even bigger difference, we realized that we needed more support, more resources. We needed to hire talented, like-minded people. But if you have ever hired a staff, you know it is not as easy as just hiring people. You need to figure where they will work, what resources they need, who will train them, and a lot of other details to foster creativity and productivity.

As Michelle and I confronted all these questions, we decided that creating a virtual company was consistent with our commitments. We both love to travel and we wanted the ability to live and work anywhere in the world. Our new staff members could work from their own home and would enjoy the same freedom to work from anywhere they wanted. It was that intention that allowed me to start writing this book in Asheville, NC; then finish it in Budapest, Hungary; Dubrovnik, Croatia; and Subotica, Serbia.

Even though we were recognized by Good Morning America for this virtual business model, it wasn't always unicorns and rainbows. There were challenges that came along with managing staff all over the country. But you know the English proverb, "Necessity is the mother of invention"?

It was clear that we had very talent and committed staff, but there was a resource that was missing. We needed a way to track results and make sure everyone was on the same page. We also wanted a tool that made our staff's job easier, a way for them to quickly pitch the media and provide everything they needed right at their fingertips. We looked into all the solutions out there and kept questioning what would really make a difference. We finally came to the conclusion that we needed to create our own solution.

So we set out to create our online press kit technology, PressKit 24/7. This was a big investment for us both in time and money. It wasn't always easy as we ventured into this techie world. But it was clear it would make a difference for our team. And it did payoff for us big time! It has been the resource that has made THE difference for our company.

Knowing what resources are needed is the key to staying in the flow. The quickest way to get unstuck is to get clear about what resource you need when you need it: coaching, training, staff, technology, or whatever. If you're not clear about the resources you need to get from here to there, you're always going to be 'here'. What resource would make THE difference? It's something you should ask yourself continually. What you need today might be completely different from what you need tomorrow.

Structure Your Day

Often entrepreneurs, especially solopreneurs, thrust themselves into a flurry of doing, doing, doing. It becomes a tornado-like swirl and it is the biggest source of overwhelm. There is so much to do and only me or my small staff to do it! Everything seems to scream at the same volume, "Do me next!" "No, do *me!*" It can create the paper shovel, where you move one unfinished document from one side of the desk to the other. You know what I am talking about. You sit there in a daze, busily working on whatever is the least confronting – insignificant tasks instead of more impactful projects.

For me, it's emails. I read and reread my emails, not really taking action on any of them. I am for sure not in pre-vacation mode. You know how it is. Right before you are about to go on vacation and you get, like, 10 years' worth of work done in an afternoon.

Not taking action on those things that are the most important to your business can leave you feeling like you're constantly trying to catch up and avert another crisis, or it can put you into a state of total action. Looking at all that screams for our attention can feel so overwhelming that we'll do anything to escape that feeling: grab a cup of coffee, feed the cat, check in on the kids – all excuses to not deal with the source of the overwhelm.

How you set the stage for your day is the most important thing you can do. It sets the tone for how that day goes and it has you get clear on your intentions. And once you are clear, the universe is right there to back you up.

I want to share how I structure my day. But, you need to find your structure, a structure that serves you and matches your rhythms and cycles. First, I set up the day. This is where I get clear about my motivation for the day. I start my day with meditation. Personally, I find I gain clarity by mediating. By putting my mind on my breath, focusing on the air coming in and coming out, I begin to stable my mind. Without all that mind chatter, there is clarity. Then I can look and see what my motivation is.

Why am I doing what I'm doing? Why am I meditating? Why am I working on this project (which recently was writing this book)? Or why am I writing this blog post? Asking "why" has transformed my conversation about writing a book and has transformed my life.

While writing this book, there were a couple of conversations I had with a dear friend (and my writing coach) that had a huge impact on me and really shifted my perception. The first was the difference between writing and editing. I realized that writing is a passion of mine. Editing? Not so much. The other conversation began as a question: "Why are you writing this book?" When Heather asked me, I started to give her an answer that many wannabe authors would give: "I have a message. I think it would make a difference. To change the world. It's a great calling card. Yadda, yadda, yadda." She stopped me and asked, "Not 'why are you writing *a* book.' Why are you writing *this* book?" *This* book? I'd never thought about it like that.

When Heather began to work with me to uncover the answer to this question, everything began to fall into place. I knew what I wanted to say, and how I wanted to say it. This shift changed everything for me.

Without being clear about the 'why' for your day, you're thrown to design your day from the past, from your To Do List that just goes on and on, and not from your commitment and what really serves your business. Remember, the motivation, or your 'why' for the day, is (big picture) your intention for the day. My daily meditations are often aligned with my current mantra: freedom through discipline, wake up and enliven the world.

With motivation identified, it is time to warm up. Great athletes always warm up. They don't just jump out of bed and onto the field right away. They have a warm up routine. Do you have a warm up routine, or do you jump right out of bed and, in one fell swoop, potty (technical term), reach for your Crackberry, switch on the computer, nod at your significant other, and you're off to the races? It all sounds well and good. The only problem is this sets you up for a tornado that leaves papers and chaos in its wake. I'm sure I am not the only one who has lived through these tornados, either one time or a million.

Just like a star athlete, you need to create your warm up plan. For me, I drink my water with lemon, I have my tea, and I meditate. When I'm calm and centered, I get present to what I call the "what's so." To get to the "what's so", I sit down and take stock of what is going on in the business, what current campaigns and projects are happening, who I need to check in with, and I identify the most important things for me to move forward that day.

I make checklists and I write it all down, so I can see it in black and white and feel like I've got a handle on "what's so." This is particularly useful when I am feeling overwhelmed. I create a road map of what there is to do and what actions I need to take, then I prioritize it. It sounds simple, but it's very powerful. By writing it down and prioritizing it, I can cut through the noise and work through what is important. Sometimes our sense of overwhelm gets us thinking that it's the end of the world. But at those times, we just need to breathe and bring things back into perspective. That full inbox might actually turn out to be only five emails needing a response. And that endless list of people you have to get back to is really just ten calls you can schedule in.

While this comes in handy when I am overwhelmed, mostly I just look over everything and sit with it until I am clear about what actions are going to make the biggest difference. Without this clarity, entrepreneurs get stuck by diving into their inbox with its constant flood of information, requests, and comments. They get overwhelmed and go into their email craziness and get sucked up by it. Or they get caught up in whatever direction the wind happens to be blowing at the time, whichever wheel is the squeakiest. But when you are clear about your priorities, you know exactly what to do next to move forward on your commitment and purpose. So I prioritize what is actually important to do at that very moment. Then I pick the three I am going to complete that day.

A number of years ago, I saw a very successful entrepreneur speak. He said that he focuses on three things he is going to get done each day – and that is it. Three things. Of course you can pick as many things as you have the ability to handle. But if you're a Type A personality (overachiever), please only pick three. Why? Since I work with a couple of those types, I see the common tendency is to make a To-Do list a mile long and then go into overwhelm! So pick three. Remember, after those three are done you can tackle as many others as you want. There is something magical that happens when you complete something. When I was just starting out working at Landmark, my manager, Diana, shared a very powerful insight. She would complete one thing before she left for work. It didn't really matter what it was, it could be as simple as making the bed. What it did was set the tone for the whole day. It's the same idea with picking three things to complete and then completing them. You'll see miracles happen when you do this. I also play a game to have the To-Do items completed before my team wakes up in the U.S.

So now that you are set up and warmed up, make sure that you have a structure to keep your head in the game. In other words, be present. When you are designing your day, come up with way to check in with yourself throughout the day to make sure that you're fully present. It can be whatever works for you: a walk, a tea break, or a quick meditation session – something simple that wakes you up and keeps you on track.

This is a powerful way to design your day: Set up your day by getting clear on your motivation, warm up by getting present to the work before you, and ask yourself, "What three things am I going to accomplish today?" Periodically, take breaks that interrupt the noise and have you get present. If you do, it will be a very successful day! Rather than reacting to the clatter and clamor of things screaming for your attention, you focus on these three things (setup, warm up, heads up) that are going to move your business and life forward.

Complementary Resources

The great Greek philosopher Socrates said, "Know thyself." I think one of the reasons entrepreneurs are entrepreneurs is because they have a deep need to know themselves. And if you really want to know yourself, one way to do that is to start a business. It has you confront all the good, bad, and ugly about yourself. But this journey to self-discovery can be one of your biggest challenges. By nature, we think we can do everything better than anybody else can, right? Come on, you know what I am talking about. That is why we went into business for ourselves. We are going to do it better. This entrepreneurial spirit is what builds empires and changes the world. But it can also create blind spots where we don't see our strengths and weaknesses. And not seeing these blind spots makes it hard to navigate.

My friend Laurie Ford once told me that a business is made up of three kinds of people: creators, managers, and completers. And to really get things done, you need all three – or you have to be all three – because every project has all three stages: launch/initiation, completion, and maintenance. If you don't understand this or pay attention to it, you'll find yourself being ineffective no matter how hard you work.

I think many entrepreneurs are creators – at least I definitely am. One of the things that gets us stuck is the hurry to just create, create, create. I'm always eager to launch new initiatives or projects, but there is no management or completion. I've learned that to really succeed and push forward with all my ideas, I need to first know what stage a project is in: Is it in the launch phase, the completion stage, or maintenance stage? By identifying the phase, I know when to get the support of other people who are managers or completers – or to access those capabilities in myself.

Generally, completers won't get caught spinning their wheels during a project like we creators do. But completers and managers may not pay enough attention to developing new programs or projects. Whatever your type, take a look at your business and its various components. Create a list of everything that's outstanding. What stage are they in? Do they need to be launched, completed, or maintained at this point in time? Put those items in the creation column, the management column, and the completion column.

Next, ask yourself if you are the best person for whatever stage they are in. If not, who is and how can you get that support? If you need to hire support for yourself, this will help you know what kind of person you need to help you so you can turn those items over to them. But if you're not in position to hire support, can you "build the muscles" of those capabilities that are not natural to you? Often, those capabilities that are not natural are also our least favorite! But they need to be done, and successful people will generally start with those things they like the least and finish with those things they love the most.

My partner at Wasabi, Michelle, and I are a good balance of alike and opposite. She is extraverted and loves to talk. I am more introverted and love to listen. I am big picture and she is detail oriented. When we designed our business, we both picked accountabilities that played to our strengths. We also looked at our experience: Michelle had the PR background and I had the marketing background. I truly believe that our differences have been the recipe for our financial success. The reason we are so fulfilled is because of our likeness. We share a similar commitment to make a difference on the planet and to support our clients to do the same. We also share a passion for the environment and animals.

Your Environment as a Resource

Too often we don't see the water we're swimming in. It's just the water. It's like when I was sliding into the hotpots with the naked hippies. I felt a tingling from the contrast of the crisp night air and the biting heat of the water. But after a while, it became the way that it was – the water was no longer hot or cold.

Take the koi fish, for example. In captivity, they grow small because they have no adversity. When in the wild, the koi face lots of adversity (like other fish wanting to eat them), so they grow larger. Also, in both Chinese and Japanese tradition, koi fish are known for swimming upstream. When faced with adversity, most fish will "go with the flow" and follow the stream. But no matter the weather conditions, no matter how hard or steep it may be, no matter how many waterfalls, the koi fish will swim upstream. This is viewed as a show of power because they will continue to swim upstream as if on a mission. They cannot be distracted or deterred by anything.

184

Or, take the goldfish. Recent reports have found monster goldfish up to 18 inches long breeding in Lake Tahoe, with the belief that they ended up there after being released into the wild by aquarium owners. In large waters, the goldfish thrive.

Too often our environment goes unquestioned and it could be the sand of your regular environment that has you stuck. Everything is FINE (and we know what that stands for). It could be the people around you, the community you live in, or the culture within which you are doing business. An environment that keeps you stuck might even include your friends and family. It's in the conversations you have and the perspective you absorb.

When you change your environment, you find yourself changing everything from your habits to how you communicate with others. If you've ever lived in a foreign country or a different part of your own country, you know that this is true. You might even pick up a new accent! A great way to know yourself is by observing yourself in other cultures.

Living in Hungary is an eye-opener for me. When we first got here, I tried to immerse myself in the business community. We hired a couple of interns because I believe the youth are a great indication of where a country is heading. Our interns blew me away. They were so talented and eager to learn. It really had me rethink a lot of what we were doing as a business. While they were great, I began to notice an interesting theme with other companies I was looking to hire. The meeting would go great and I was clear I wanted to hire them – then there would be no follow up from them. I would send an email thanking them and letting them know exactly what we needed, and nothing. It was so weird.

Curious, I asked Teo (our star intern) what that was all about. She explained that they don't have the same relationship to business that we do in the U.S. Failure is not an option for them, so unlike in America, where the entrepreneurial spirit is part of our fabric, it is not so for them. So they approach business very cautiously. Interestingly, you can see the result of their dancing to this conversation.

It makes you begin to question the conversations (environment) *you're* dancing to. People in general gravitate to their comfort zones. Sometimes we need to see the contrast in order to notice the water. We live in neighborhoods that feel consistent with who we perceive ourselves to be and we have friends who think like we do. But as an entrepreneur, you can't afford to be too comfortable. You need the edge of fresh, new ideas and people who inspire you – even as they intimidate you a little! If you live in a culture that is complacent (as many would argue the U.S. is becoming), you need to relate to that segment of the population that isn't complacent (i.e. recent immigrants). In general, you need to branch out of your comfort zone.

By pushing the envelope and looking for the contrast, you can create a positive, uplifting, energetic, gung-ho environment that makes a huge positive difference to you and your business.

Surrounding yourself with people who believe in you and who root for your success is not only more fun, but it encourages you to become what they see in you. Even being in a setting that is beautiful to you can lift your spirits and keep you from getting down and stuck!

As a fun exercise, look inside your community of people: do you have the same conversations over and over, and are those conversations limiting or empowering you?

Entrepreneur, author, and business philosopher Jim Rohn said, "You are the average of the five people you spend the most time with." So if you want to increase your income, start interacting with people who make the kind of money you want to make and have the kind of success you wish to have. I promise you, these people are talking about different issues and in a totally different way than people who are struggling to make ends meet.

Just like with the koi fish, adversity and contrast provide opportunities to see the water that we are swimming in and let us know if it's time to change the water, or to simply swim upstream.

Technology

Don't you just love technology when it works... when it doesn't, not so much? It doesn't much matter if you love technology or not, because it's an important, structural aspect we all face as entrepreneurs. And if you don't keep up with the rapid pace, you are going to fall behind. In just a few decades, the internet has forever changed the face of business, making dissemination of information easier than ever before. But it can be a double-edged sword. New technology can be overwhelming. The huge selection of onsite marketing tools and online outlets can be totally confusing. Sometimes it's so boggling to figure out what direction to move in that it's easier to just avoid the whole decision-making process. Even with my technical background, I sometimes find it daunting to wade through the technology choices that are available to us and our clients. In other words, when it comes to technology, it's easy for any of us to get stuck.

If technology has you shaking your head, I think breaking the problem into manageable chunks can really help. But to get it right, you need to start by asking some of the biggest or most fundamental questions. (And if you're really feeling stuck in general, these are questions you might have been avoiding!) For example, what are the ultimate goals of your business? Your message? Who are you trying to reach? Identifying your professional mission and your audience may seem overly simplistic, but it's a surprisingly effective shortcut to figuring out what technology is going to make the biggest difference for you.

Technology is often the answer to a structural challenge you and your business are facing. In one of my trainings, I counseled a woman who works as an intuitive. Traditionally, she had worked with clients one-on-one. But she felt stuck in that modality and wanted to work with larger groups. She couldn't figure out the transition piece, exactly how she could get from one-on-one sessions into something bigger. In her case, I saw that technology (specifically, Skype video conferencing) could help her build a bridge to that next level. Using Skype, she could design a multi-person program that she could deliver to six or eight people at a time. Skype is a free technology, so the only investment she had to make was of her own time and energy to develop a group format. It was the perfect next step for her, and she continues to hone her program using Skype. In her case, technology provided the exact platform she needed to get moving again with her vision. It was not the solution for her ultimate goal, but it was her perfect next step.

Often I see people wanting to jump from A to Z, trying to skip the steps in between rather than creating structures as they go along. So they leap ahead of themselves and create a technology or business structure for working with hundreds of clients. Really, the next step for them should be creating a structure that can transition them to taking bigger steps. You don't want to get overwhelmed by building a structure that is too big for you. It won't help you move forward any faster and may actually sabotage everything you're trying to create. I speak from experience and from seeing other people take on technology that leaves them so overwhelmed they don't use it at all.

But Lynn was very clear on her resources. She was clear that she didn't have a lot of money to invest. So we looked at a structure that was free. She was clear that she had a possible resource that she could use for her next step toward fulfilling on what she was committed to and delivering her passion.

It is better to expand gradually rather than making huge leaps that leave you overwhelmed and frustrated. That isn't to say that someday Lynn won't be leading conferences of a hundred people or more, as was her original vision when we first spoke. In fact, I have no doubt that will be the case, at least if that's where she decides she still wants to go. But without creating an interim structure, one that felt a little closer to her original existing paradigm of the one-on-one format, she would have been trying to do so without a safety net.

Collaboration versus Competition

It's ironic that we have so much, yet we live in a world of scarcity. We're constantly being told the world is coming to an end; watch your back; people are out to get you; take advantage of your (fill in the blank). So we run around frantically. We have become hoarders in some form or another and we've forgotten how to work together. In this illusion, we've reverted to our primal instincts. It's the survival of the fittest and we have to knock each other down in order to survive. We get caught up in fierce competition to get on top where it's supposedly safe.

It is easy to fall into this mindset because there is a lot of agreement. We think we have a limited market and the only way to make a sale is to outdo the next guy. But what if we changed our mindset? What if we saw the world as abundant and not limited? What if we all would find more success by succeeding together? What if we actually developed a way to collaborate with others for a mutual win-win?

When we focus on those things that we're really committed to and not beating out someone else, the world opens so many more doors. We have this mistaken impression that there is a lack of business so we turn other people into competitors. But if you really stop to think about it, there are so many opportunities out there. No one really needs to be fighting for the scraps.

What I always try to do, even if it looks like I am meeting a competitor, is look for ways we can work together that will be a win-win. Sometimes there are, sometimes there aren't; but I like to evaluate each opportunity. It opens you to the global citizen mentality and global markets, a world that works for everybody. There are enough resources on the planet if we just have collaboration versus competition.

For example, as I write this I am in Hungary meeting with other PR firms. These firms specialize in getting people into the European market. Wasabi specializes in getting people into the American market. Though we also get clients into the Euro market all the time, we can give our clients more options if we partner with these other firms. By doing this, I'm not trying to go against the grain, but trying to find ways to establish myself in a new market and learn from people who are already successful there. One of the best ways to benefit your business is to make contacts.

Once you start looking for ways to collaborate with people, you can provide clients a much broader range of service. When someone chooses a large company over a smaller firm, one of the reasons is the bigger menu of services and options large companies offer with multiple people, personalities, skillsets, and experience. By collaborating with other small firms, you can offer this breadth as well.

So think about how you can collaborate with others. For us, a great example is book publicity. At Wasabi, we don't do book publicity per se. We work with clients who want to be seen as an expert and position that expertise inside the media, which is completely different from book publicity. We recently hired a book publicist to handle book tours for us. By partnering with others, we can now offer all the services that a large firm can. We can assemble a campaign that has the very best people working on it, the top of the food chain.

Inner Resources

We've talked a lot about mindsets and how they leave you spinning your wheels, stuck in the sand. But there are also mindsets that can help you thrive as an entrepreneur. I call these your inner resources and they are as important – or more so! – than your human and financial resources. Just like those external resources, it's important to make sure your inner resources are in place and ready to support you. In my own personal and professional life, the inner resources I pay

196

particular attention to are balance, knowing, and

focus/awareness.

BALANCE

Your business and personal life are like yin and yang. Each is interconnected and interdependent of each other. If you let one area take more control in your life, you're bound to feel out of balance. Spend too long in imbalance and eventually you'll get stuck. I know that to keep my life in synch means keeping true to all my commitments. If I don't, I start to feel unsatisfied and edgy. Through this book, you've already defined your purpose, your values, and what is important to you. Holistic awareness interweaves those things with all areas of your life. Rather than dividing your attention and focusing on one piece of life at a time, that sense of holistic awareness is like the bird's eye view of your life that taps into a higher consciousness. Through this lens, your happiness flows through each and everything you do.

I have a lot of commitments in my life, but each plays a role in how I work and affects how I interact with others and how I feel about myself. And I now know that being stuck comes in all forms and shapes. It could be the smallest thing throwing you off and you wouldn't even know it. Your life doesn't always wave great big red flags, so it's important to sense when you no longer feel at ease in any part of your life. For example, an unpleasant interaction with a vendor could make you cranky with your pets when you get home. If you didn't notice the source, you could easily get stuck in a crummy mood for the entire evening.

Sometimes it's not the external world that is dragging you down. It could be your most familiar setting, your body. These days, I see so many people running out of steam by the end of the day or even before. They have their purpose in life, but their energy has been completely zapped and they're not able to do all the things they would like to do. One of the easiest things to do is to listen to your body.

I know this isn't new information. You have heard it before. Lord knows how many times I've heard it! But I see so many people trying to run their bodies on energy drinks that I don't think that the message has been heard loud and clear. It took me long enough to actually take a spoon full of my own medicine. My body and I love each other now, but we've had a tumultuous relationship.

My relationship with my body started out really great. I was a happy and healthy kid. I ate like a horse. But when I hit my teens and got strep throat a number of times, I knew I needed to start listening to my body and do what made me feel good. I can't even begin to tell you all the crazy things I did. I tried a low carb diets, Atkins, Eat Right 4 Your Type, no grains, no dairy, carb specific diets, and even a combination of these. I tried all kinds of supplements as well as drugs, both legal and illegal.

But, in the end, whatever I did made me feel stuck. It felt like an upward battle, until finally I found a staple that eased my body: meditation. I learned to naturally cleanse myself by focusing my breath and clearing my mind. That's what I needed to quiet the constant chatter of my OCD. Not only did it transform my body physically, it calmed me mentally and spiritually. Instead of finding something that gave me what I thought my body needed, practicing meditation drained me of everything I didn't need. Meditation isn't for everyone; but for me at least, it truly has been an amazing tool for nurturing my body, improving my personal life, and benefiting my business.

Too often people over-think and are so stressed at work that they forget to take good care of themselves. But it's a matter of realizing that your business and personal life are all part of the same system. If one is off kilter, the other will be affected accordingly. I feed my body and my mind what it needs so both my business and personal lives thrive. Don't sacrifice your commitments, because they are as essential to you as any other life decision. Don't throw away your hobbies or write off going on your routine run.

When you start forgetting to do the small things, your body and mind start to take the toll, which then leads to bigger, unnecessary problems. My father is a very wise man. His theory as to why we are on this planet is to learn to be in our physical bodies. If you stop and think about this, it makes a lot of sense. You know the saying, that we are all spiritual beings, having a physical experience?

From the very beginning of working with Michelle, our business journey has been wrapped up in our physical journey. We launched our business while we were doing Bill Phillips' Body For Life program. (I wanted to include my before and after picture here, but I looked so hot my book would have to be sold in the adult section – just joking of course!) What we have learned though this whole journey is if we're physically off, our business is off. Just like in business, great health is a journey – not a destination.

The Dance

So we've been talking a lot about you and your career, but your life isn't only about your career. Like a river, all tributaries of your life flow into one main channel. I know I wouldn't be satisfied with my career if I was working on a fixed day-to-day schedule. I need flexibility in my life. That's why I love being in Budapest. My schedule is perfect. It fits both my personal passions and my work life. I wake up to 3:00 a.m. Eastern Time and head out to explore the city and markets. We shop at the great market hall and stroll along the Danube, or grab a leisurely lunch. After a relaxing morning (remember, this is EVERY day), it's time to prepare for my clients, get down to business, and start my workday, which means sitting on the couch and turning on my computer. It's the perfect structure for me to be productive and fulfilled.

On my first extended stay in Hungary, I was loving life. But as happy as I was, I knew there was still something missing from my life in Budapest. I realized quickly that without Brodee and

Bailey, our two spaniels, our family wasn't complete. For those of you who aren't pet people, I know this sounds crazy. But our dogs are essential to my happiness. I knew I had to figure out how to bring them over to Hungary or I wasn't going to feel completely happy with my life, either personally or business-wise. I mean, who was I going to consult with when my staff was driving me crazy?

So, what did I do? I became obsessed, searching for every way possible to transport the dogs from the U.S. to Europe. I really didn't want them flying in the cargo area of a plane, so we looked into flying them on a private transport. There was an article in the New York Times that talked about how, if you found an empty leg on a private flight, it could be as cheap as flying first class. Bingo. So I found a couple of companies that sell these empty legs.

I was a little shocked when I got a quote of $77,000 to fly from Atlanta to Amsterdam (not the city I wanted to fly out of or fly into). Let's just say that was a little more than I wanted to spend. The other option was taking a transatlantic cruise on the RMS Queen Mary II, but the schedule didn't work.

I finally stumbled onto Lufthansa and learned they actually fly the dogs in a separate area that is pressurized, just like where the humans sit. The only difference is they get to lie down. In short, it all worked out! I'm not sure if my dogs love the city like I love the city; navigating the concrete and crazy people is much different than strolls through the forest. But all the new smells are a bonus.

So, ask yourself, in all the areas of your life, what things are most important to you? This can range from your career, to your spirituality, to your friends or intimate relationships, to perhaps, most importantly, your pets (I know I am one of those people). Sometimes we get so caught up in the swirl of things that we let the business side of our lives take over and forget what is most important to us outside of our work. We may have chosen to be entrepreneurs because of the freedom, but we sometimes end up getting shackled to our work.

When you take a step back and really consider what you want most for your life and business, everything will start to flow more smoothly. Think about the places in your life where you are not fully participating. Where do you feel disconnected? Have you been spending less time with your family or friends, or maybe a favorite passion of yours? Although your career may be in the forefront, you need a time and place to recharge your batteries. So go play with your kids, take your significant other out, go for a run, sing in the shower, have a glass of wine, go to a museum, read a great book (*not* business related!) – anything that revitalizes you and makes you feel alive and human again! Who knew that a great glass of wine could keep you from hitting a roadblock? Remember everything in life, even the smaller things, contribute to your overall happiness. Often they are the most important!

About Inner Knowing

I once thought, "You have got to be kidding me! Sit still and focus on my breath for 30 minutes? Really? This doesn't seem logical. How is trying to be quiet going to make any difference with my OCD? When I try to meditate, all I can hear are my thoughts. A lot of them!"

I turned to meditation because I was looking for answers about my OCD and my overall well-being. I tried meditation off and on throughout my life. It didn't seem to make much of a difference. I couldn't figure out what all the fuss was about. I would give it a go and sit there thinking to myself, "This is crazy! It's not relaxing me at all. All I am doing is getting more tense. This is so boring." Those thoughts would go on and on until I would decide it was crazy and I'd give up. I really can't remember what had me turn to it one more time.

Maybe my OCD was out of hand or life was particularly challenging, but for whatever reason I showed up on the steps of the Shambhala Meditation Center of Asheville to take a beginner course in meditation. Something clicked. I heard for the first time that meditation was a journey and all those thoughts were a good thing. They were opportunities to place my focus back on the breath, to be present. I finally got it! The name of the game is being present.

The interesting thing was the more I practiced sitting on my cushion and quieting my mind, the more I noticed being present in life. That focusing on my breath and the air hitting the top of my nasal cavity on the inhale with total relaxation on the exhale during my meditation helped me get more present. With each breath, the constant chatting in my mind grew quieter and quieter until finally it stopped. I became connected to all of it. Only then could I hear like I'd never heard before, as if my body was talking to me. Sure, before this, my body told me when it was hungry and when it was thirsty. But I missed the subtle nuances, the signals that mean the difference between surviving and thriving in life.

I could finally hear my voice and that voice began to speak to me throughout the day. I'm not talking about that endless chatter and nonsense that normally filled my head, that crummy little voice that was constantly complaining. It is a knowing. You know what I'm talking about. Those moments where the fogs lifts and, in its wake, you are left with calm, clarity, and certainty.

Focus versus Attachment

Entrepreneurs often confuse focus with attachment. One of the common pitfalls for entrepreneurs is getting attached to a particular outcome rather than letting the universe unfold as it will. When you become attached to something, the energy stops flowing. I see this all the time working with my clients. They get attached to a particular outcome that has to look and be a certain way rather than letting it unfold as the universe intends it to. This can be a huge roadblock because you're being a stubborn bull. It's your way or the highway. Not only does that leave you frustrated and stuck, it leaves the people working with you and for you stuck. You close yourself from anyone else's perspective and only see one road leading you to the finish line.

I think what most people fear is that if they let go they'll feel lost and uncertain about what to do next. But that's never the case. You will always have your purpose, values, and what's important to guide you in the right direction. Letting go doesn't mean losing control. You can stay focused and intentional, but you keep open the possibilities. If you get too attached to a specific outcome, you'll often miss great opportunities appearing in front of you. Or your expectations are so high that you are let down in the end – even if the outcome is amazing. In fact, by holding specific expectations about an event in life rather than staying open and aware of the good that life creates, you become frustrated and stuck.

A perfect example of this is my recent experience at a Hungarian Starbucks. As a professed coffee addict, I knew the drill. I went up to the counter to order my grande café latte (my drug of choice – two raw sugars, please) and waited patiently to pick it up. Well, Starbucks is a recent phenomenon in

Budapest and this one had just opened. But still I expected it to be the same experience I'd always had in the States.

Standing in line in front of me that morning was an older, obviously confused Hungarian woman trying to order. She and the barista got into a heated discussion. I don't speak a lick of Hungarian, so couldn't quite figure out the issue. But the woman eventually left, looking upset and confused about what was probably a standard Starbucks-issue cappuccino (much larger than a typical European shot-sized cappuccino).

When I ordered my coffee just like my zillions of other Starbucks orders, I definitely saw the sense of relief on the barista's face. He saw that I knew what to do in this place. He then asked for my name – Drew. Uh oh. "What?" he asked. The name "Drew" was nowhere in his experience and he was perplexed trying to figure it out. Not only that, but the confused Hungarian woman returned to the counter to continue ranting. That's when things got interesting. The whole staff came scurrying to see what the problem was and the barista seemed to be having a mental meltdown.

At that point, I stepped out of the way until they worked it all out. But I knew this wasn't how it was supposed to work! You order your drink, they take your money, and then you proceed to pick it up at the counter. Didn't these Hungarians get the memo? Eventually, the eager barista, who was not so eager anymore, was so flustered that he didn't even look up to hand me the receipt. This was definitely not the Starbucks experience that I know and love.

But here's the problem. Everyone in this situation was attached to their expectations. The older Hungarian woman was so fixated on what she expected she couldn't simply enjoy the coffee without disrupting the rest of the service. The barista and the rest of the Starbucks team were so attached to trying to please this one woman that the awesome customer service that Starbucks is known for got tossed out the window.

And I recognized that my own attachment issues were alive and kicking. I know exactly how I like my coffee and have been a dedicated Starbucks customer for what seems like forever. Just like that old Hungarian woman who wanted her traditional cappuccino, I wanted my grande café latte without any drama. By being so attached to how it was usually served, I completely forgot about my commitment to always being great with people in any given situation.

When you get fixated on a specific result, you lose sight of your most important commitments. If you focus on your purpose and commitments, the correct and perfect results will appear. But if you focus on specific results, your original purpose and commitments tend to get lost.

What we need to do as entrepreneurs is to show up, give it 100%, play the game fully, and accept what we get. When we are attached, we show up but we are not really giving it 100%. We're wearing the blinders that our expectations created and we are not seeing the whole perspective.

Letting Go Exercise

When entrepreneurs are attached,

we sometimes get into tantrums.

You know what I am talking about!

Like little kids, we only want what

we want and we want it done our

way! If we don't get it, we get fussy

and out of sorts. Once we start feeling that way, it becomes a

downward spiral. Not only does that leave us unhappy, but it

closes us off from other opportunities and weighs us down.

A good way to experience this is to grab a couple of friends and

play a game of tug-of-war. Or if you are too grown up and

dignified, just play this game in your head. One side represents

your business while the other side represents that single result

you've been fixated on. The game usually starts with both sides

evenly pulling their weight. It looks like the rope is at a

standstill, but really both teams are pulling with all their might.

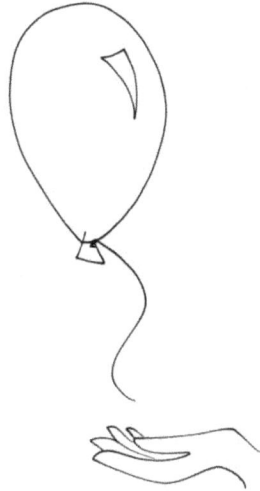

But as we know from gym class, it's the team who pulls the hardest that wins, right?

With that simple goal in mind, we all become competitive – really competitive. Sometimes being competitive and working towards goals gives you a great sense of accomplishment especially if you win. But sometimes blind ambition and the need to win leads to dubious behavior. Plus it's a lot of arm-straining, teeth-grinding work! Is winning the only possible option? What if you weren't fixated on winning? You could always decide to change the rules of the game and just let go of the rope!

What happens then? Based on the basic laws of physics, letting go of your end of the rope will send the other team tumbling and falling on their rear ends. Not only is this funny, but now you finally get to rest those tired arms of yours! And, once you stop playing, there is a new perspective that you don't need to play that game. You might find something better to do than tugging at a rope.

216

So think of your business is the same way. Maybe you've been too fixated on things being or looking a certain way. It might be that you've gotten so attached to a certain set of results that it's even prevented you from winning the overall game. Sometimes the best thing to do is to simply let go of that fixated result, drop those blinders, and see what else is out there. When you become attached to something, it stops the natural flow of energy. You're in that standstill position in a game of tug-of-war where you're using all your strength but the rope just isn't budging either way – and you find yourself stuck. So take on the challenge of letting things go.

Measure your Success

What business game are you playing? This may be an odd question, but to be clear, business is a game. If you aren't clear on the rules of the game, how are you ever going to know if you've won? It would be very confusing to play Monopoly with Yahtzee rules. And it's the same for you: if you are playing the 'make a difference' game but using the 'make a lot of money' game rules, does that make sense? For most of us, the answer is not "do those things that cause you to generate more revenue" but "do those things that help you grow as a human being."

When Michelle and I created Wasabi, we were clear we wanted to make a difference. We also saw that we could make a bigger impact on the world by supporting others who had that same commitment. By empowering them to get their message out into the world, we would change what people are talking about. And by changing what people are talking about, we could help to change the world. In order for us to win the game, we had to make a difference.

Now, of course, that's not the whole story. There are other universal rules that apply to every game of business. And the rule that drives people the most nutty is about money: you need to make it in order to even play the game of business. Michelle and I could have gone another route to make a difference, but we chose business. So, let's talk about this thing that drives everyone crazy. I remember being stuck when I heard someone say that the amount of money you make is directly related to the amount of energy you are putting out in the world. That changed everything for me. When you think about playing the game from this perspective, don't you notice you begin to feel free? All that noise about making money begins to quiet, and it becomes simple. If you want different results, all you need to do is put more energy out into the world.

I believe there is another chapter to this story. That not only is it about the amount of energy, but also *what* energy. Too often the energy we have around money is fear because we have it so wrapped up in our measure of success. If you want to see miracles, transform the very powerful energy of fear into something else – action, love, creation – and put that out in the world. But it's not all about more, more, more. We get so caught up in the mentality that we are not successful unless we get more clients, make more money, beat out the competition.

For me, that's not what business is about. It's about being fulfilled, being present. But in order to know if we are winning the game, we have to figure out for ourselves "When is enough, enough?" If you don't know where enough is for yourself as an entrepreneur, you'll find yourself in an endless grind.

To me, happiness and fulfillment go hand in hand. I don't know that you can really have one without the other. Psychologist Abraham Maslow theorized that human beings have a hierarchy of needs. The most basic needs are physical survival and safety. When those needs are met, we focus on love and community, then self-esteem. The highest level is self-actualization. For the most part, most of us entrepreneurs have all of our basic needs met. We're really at the place where we should be self-actualizing. As we discussed in the beginning of this book, that is why a lot of entrepreneurs are stuck. They have all the stuff that should make them happy, but they're stuck. They're unfulfilled and unhappy in life. I can relate. Been there, done that. Let me paint you a picture . . .

I really had the good life. I had an amazing job. I had the physical ability and the freedom and financial ability to travel and do what I wanted. But I still had this feeling of slogging through the mud in life. It wasn't complete. "I've hit a wall and can't move" kind of stuck. But I was just kind of going along. I saw that even though I had all this stuff, I wasn't really feeling that I was happy and fulfilled and satisfied. I think many people these days have that same kind of feeling. They're just not fully connected to life. They're disconnected and just going through the motions. They're kind of numb to life – and so was I. Thankfully, I woke up so I could dream again.

Waking up to Dream

In 1961, John F. Kennedy announced that we were going to put a man on the moon. We didn't have the technology and nobody knew how this was going to happen, but he said this shall be. And it was. He had a dream, just like Martin Luther King: a picture of a world that others couldn't see themselves inside of, a new reality.

Dreaming with purpose wakes us up. It gets the blood flowing. The conversation in our head gets noisy. But underneath it all, there is a calm, an inner knowing. This is meant to be.

Most of us have forgotten how to dream with purpose. And we confuse the daydreaming that we do to avoid life, someday, one day, fantasizing with truly dreaming. Dreaming with purpose.

So what is dreaming with purpose? It is when you create a picture where you actually see yourself taking actions that move you toward your dream. You are creating a plan, a way to fulfill your purpose. It's an active vision – not just a vague pie in the sky fantasy that you say you want but you don't pursue.

One of my favorite shows is House Hunters International. The crew follows people around the world who are looking for homes to buy in foreign countries. When I started watching the show, I began daydreaming about how nice it would be if someday we had a house in another country. At that stage, it was a very passive fantasy.

It all shifted when I began to dream with purpose and actually decided to make it happen. I started thinking about what countries we might like and I considered what it would take to actually fulfill my dream. I thought about how to book travel, research the real estate market, and, as I mentioned, how I was going to get my animals over there. Hungary popped up as a strong candidate. I created a list. I began to do research on the internet to explore what the real estate market was like and what other people said about it and what problems they confronted. At this stage, I was dreaming with purpose. I didn't know how I was going to make it happen. All I knew was that it WAS going to happen.

One of my favorite movies is Under the Tuscan Sun. If you haven't seen it, rent it! On the surface, the film is your typical chick flick (which I happen to be a big fan of). But if you look deeper, there are some very profound messages. It's just like eating a meal that you think is just like all the others. But if you really get present to the food, you can taste the subtle, life-altering flavors.

The story goes like this. After finding out her husband is having an affair, Frances (Diane Lane), a book critic, ends up on a romantic tour of Tuscany all alone. During one of the stops, while wandering the streets of Cortona, she sees an advertisement for a villa for sale. She rejoins her tour on the bus and, just outside the town, the bus makes an unexpected stop to allow a herd of sheep to cross the road. Frances realizes they've stopped right in front of the villa she had seen in the posting earlier that day. Frances believes it's a sign, and immediately buys the home.

One of the most profound scenes is a conversation she has with her Realtor, Martini. Frances is questioning herself, naturally, thinking how crazy she is to buy a villa in a foreign country that needs a lot of TLC. In the scene, she's crying, asking herself out loud why she bought the huge house for only her, for a life she doesn't have. Martini shares a powerful story:

"Signora, between Austria and Italy, there is a section of the Alps called the Semmering. It is an impossibly steep, very high part of the mountains. They built a train track over these Alps to connect Vienna and Venice. They built these tracks even before there was a train in existence that could make the trip. They built it because they knew some day, the train would come."

Whether or not this story is true, it has you stop and ponder.

When we were packing up our house in the U.S. to move to Budapest, I had the exact same feelings as Frances: "What the ^$%# are we thinking? Am I sure about this?" We were leaving our beautiful house in the mountains (that we built), putting it on the vacation rental market, and moving into a 700 square foot apartment while we attempted to renovate, from floor to ceiling, an apartment in a foreign country. Genius!

In some moments the noise was louder than others – like when we had a production company filming us checking the dog kennel for our flight across the Atlantic Ocean. But even in those deafening times, those times where the noise in your head drowns out everything else, I knew that we were doing the right thing.

This was my track across the Alps.

Sometimes it's scary to trust the unknown, to keep the faith. But I believe that when the universe presents a possibility, it lets us know we are the one to carry the torch and that it's the right thing to do.

Too often, entrepreneurs and change agents listen to that noise and think it means they shouldn't lay the track until the train is built. But what would the world be like if Gandhi or Martin Luther King Jr. had waited? The world needs to get across the Alps. And although the train to take us there might not have arrived, we all need to be building those tracks. If the train is already built, I assert that you are not dreaming with purpose.

The purposeful dream also can't not be all about all about you – though sometimes we would like it to be! This became clear to me as I began to dream with purpose about owning property in a different part of the world.

As the CEO of Wasabi, it has always been my commitment that we make a difference on a global level. That the clients we work with have a commitment to change the world, not just the U.S. And while we do international PR for our clients, I also had a commitment to work with clients who were interested in making a difference here in the U.S. As I began to dream with purpose, I could see how my purpose and the company's purpose could be fulfilled in my dream.

There are three key components to dreaming with purpose. First, you don't know initially how the dream is going to get accomplished. Second, it cannot be ALL about you. Finally, you actively see your purpose being fulfilled in your dream.

Dream with Purpose Exercise

Step 1: Dream Big. First and foremost, you have to get clear on your dream; what is your intention for the outcome and how does it fit into your commitments and purpose? You don't need to know, and will most likely not know, how it's going to get accomplished. Remember, it needs to be big. What is the wildest thing you've ever dreamed of?

Step 2: This is important: your purposeful dream cannot be all about you. How will your dream fulfill your purpose? Begin to explore and play with all the possibilities.

Step 3: Create an action plan to fulfill on your purpose and your intention. Remember, you must actively see your purpose being fulfilled in the dream.

LIFE BY DESIGN

The whole purpose of getting yourself unstuck is so you can live a fulfilled life – the life that you're committed to living, making the difference you're committed to making, and fulfilling on your purpose for being here on the planet. If you're stuck, it's not an accident that you're stuck. There's actually a design and an order to it. Those areas where you are stuck are the opportunities for you to learn the life lessons that you chose to learn when you entered this planet.

The truth is, getting stuck and working with that stuckness, and ultimately getting unstuck, is really your life's work. It's the work to be done. It's the same work that's being done when people meditate. It's there to help us wake up from the dream and begin living a life that we love and that we were *meant* to live.

As I discussed early on, you know that you're unstuck because you are in the flow, in the zone. It feels right. Everything is aligned, not only for yourself, but for those people around you. You're in synch with the universe. The right resources or the right people are showing up at the right time for you and you're just kind of 'in the flow'. You're on your path.

It doesn't mean that obstacles won't come down your path. But you know how to powerfully deal with those obstacles. You may see that there is something in the middle of the road, but you know you're unstuck when it occurs as an opportunity, rather than a problem. For example, if you have a client who's unhappy or a co-worker who's unpleasant, you look at it as an opportunity to grow and expand, versus a problem that sends you into a tailspin. How can you improve your service and exceed that client's expectations? How can you relate to that co-worker in a way that is positive and nurturing for both of you? It is an opportunity to be of service.

Getting Unstuck: The Short Cut!

Let's be honest: we all love a short cut. So here is the quick road to getting unstuck. If you are stuck, you are making it all about *you*. Period. One of the most valuable lessons I've learned in life is if I am suffering, it is because the attention is on *me*. This is good news! If you want to get unstuck, just shift your attention to others.

Be of Service

Buddhism taught me if I want to be happy, I need to shift my focus from myself to serving others. To be honest, at first, it felt a little awkward. Put my mind on my breath so all beings could be happy? What did I have to do with their happiness? What about *my* happiness?

I would assert that if you look at your life and your business, those moments when you're truly happy are probably moments when your attention is off yourself and focused on other people, on what is going to make *them* happy. Ultimately, that's actually what's going to make you happy. I think this is particularly important for entrepreneurs. If you're working by yourself or you're working with a small number of people, it's easy to become self-absorbed: "What actions can I do to serve *me*? How can I make *my* business grow? How can *I* be successful?" But by just shifting a little of that attention to other people, it will shift your whole business and it will put you on flow of the universe.

So what are your specific opportunities to serve other people? Answering that question led me to become truly happy and satisfied inside my business. My business completely shifted.

I looked for ways to serve our clients and our communities – like the members of PitchRate.com, our free online leads service that connects media with experts committed to changing the world. I decided that making myself and Michelle available to answer any questions would make a difference for

232

them and the world. So we began hosting unplugged and unscripted calls where PitchRate members could ask us any questions they had. I found those calls began to get me unstuck and brought a whole new clarity to our business.

What actions could you be taking on a daily basis to shift the attention away from you and onto others?

Be Grateful

Another shortcut to getting unstuck is to enter a state of appreciation and gratitude. It's that acknowledgement in the present moment of all you have and all you've done. It's when you wake up in the morning and you just notice that you're grateful for your pillow, how comfortable your bed is, the feel of the sheets, and the warmth of blanket. You're grateful that you are able to get up and do what you love to do and what you're passionate about. You're appreciative of things that people do for you and just who they are. The experience becomes even fuller when you also acknowledge your gratitude out loud, letting people know that you appreciate them. Have you noticed how the simplest appreciation can completely turn your day around? Extend that energy and see it come back to you!

Be Present!

Unfortunately, most of us will head down the wrong road at some time or other. Isn't that why you're reading this book? But that's okay. When heading to the Tibetan stupa, from time to time, we're going get stuck in the sand. We are going to push on the gas and spin our tires, hoping that's going to get us out of the mess we're in... all the while, knowing it's just getting us stuck further. But, hopefully, you'll pick up this book, let your foot off the gas, get out of the car, and notice that you're in the most beautiful place imaginable – life! I promise you'll get present to the moment.

Look around and enjoy the vista. You *know* that your destiny is heading down that road.

ABOUT DREW GERBER

For 30 years, Drew Gerber has been inspiring those who want to change the world. As the CEO of Wasabi Publicity, lauded by the likes of PR Week and Good Morning America, he sparks "aha" conversations that lead to personal and business success. His PR firm, Wasabi Publicity, Inc., is known for landing clients on Dr. Phil, Oprah, Anderson Cooper, The Wall Street Journal, Inc., Entrepreneur, and other top media outlets.

Drew Gerber lives to launch conversations that make a difference and change the world. Join him at DestinationAha.com, where his love of conversations that make a difference and his passions for travel and PR intersect.

www.ingramcontent.com/pod-product-compliance
Lightning Source LLC
LaVergne TN
LVHW051502080426
835509LV00017B/1871